Helping Teens Work Through Grief

Second Edition

Helping Teens Work Through Grief

Second Edition

Mary Kelly Perschy

Brunner-Routledge
Taylor & Francis Group

NEW YORK AND HOVE

Published in 2004 by
Brunner-Routledge
29 West 35th Street
New York, NY 10001
www.brunner-routledge.com

Published in Great Britain by
Brunner-Routledge
27 Church Road
Hove, East Sussex
BN3 2FA
www.brunner-routledge.co.uk

10 9 8 7 6 5 4 3 2 1

Cover image: images.com/CORBIS
Cover design: Elise Weinger

Library of Congress Cataloging-in-Publication Data

Perschy, Mary Kelly, 1942–
    Helping teens work through grief / by Mary Kelly Perschy.— 2nd ed.
        p. cm.
Includes bibliographical references and index.
    ISBN 0-415-94696-4 (pbk.)
  1. Grief in adolescence.   2. Bereavement in adolescence.   3.
Teenagers—Counseling of.   4. Grief therapy.   I. Title.
    BF724.3.G73P47   2004
    155.9'37'0835—dc22
                                                2003019898

To the many teens
who have shared the turmoil of their grief

and

to those teens who are willing to
enter into that struggle,

that their pain may be healed
and may they experience a renewed life

To those adults who care enough to
support teens in their journey through grief

Contents

Part A
Understanding Grieving Teens and How to Support Them

Part B
The Teen Grief Group

Part D
Resource Material

List of Activity Sheets

List of Figures

Acknowledgments

Special gratitude to the following authors and publishers for permission to use material:

From "Amy and Mr. Matthews," by Yvonne Williams. Copyright © 1999, published by *Bereavement Magazine*.

From *Breaking the Silence: A Guide to Help Children with Complicated Grief—Suicide, Homicide, AIDS, Violence, and Abuse*, by Linda Goldman. Copyright © 1996, published by Taylor & Francis.

From *Children and Grief*, by J. William Worden. Copyright © 1996 published by Guilford Press.

From "Complications in Mourning Traumatic Death," by Therese A. Rando, in *Living with Grief After Sudden Loss: Suicide, Homicide, Accident, Heart Attack, Stroke*; edited by Ken Doka. Copyright © 1996, published by Taylor & Francis.

From *The Focusing Steps*, by Peter Campbell and Edwin McMahon. Copyright © 1991, Peter Campbell, PhD, and Edwin McMahon, PhD, published by Sheed and Ward.

From "Gathering Grieving Families: Three Activities," in *The Forum*, by Kathy Allen, Mary Perschy, and Mary Richardson. Copyright © 2002, published by Association for Death Education and Counseling.

From "'Goodbye' Means Ouch!," in *The Stress Examiner*, by Nancy Tubesing and Donald Tubesing. Copyright © 1983, published by Whole Person Associates.

From *Healing a Teen's Grieving Heart: 100 Practical Ideas for Families, Friends, and Caregivers*, by Alan D. Wolfelt. Copyright © 2001, published by Companion Press.

From *Help for the Hard Times: Getting Through Loss*, by Earl Hipp. Copyright © 1995, published by Hazelden.

From "Helping Bereaved Adolescents" by S. J. Flemming and R. Adolph, in *Adolescence and Death*, edited by C. Corr and J. McNeil. Copyright © 1986, published by Springer Publishing Company.

From *Mind, Music, and Imagery: Unlocking Your Creative Potential* (2nd ed.), by Stephanie Merritt. Copyright 1996, published by Aslan Publishing.

From "My Mind, Emotions, and Soul Matured . . . Too Fast for My Years," by Stephanie Frank. Copyright © 2000, Stephanie Frank, published by *The Washington Post*.

From "Positive Outcomes of Adolescents' Experience With Grief," in *Journal of Adolescent Research*, by Kevin Oltjenbruns. Copyright © 1991, published by Sage Publications.

From "Public Tragedy and Complicated Mourning," by Therese A. Rando, in *Living with Grief: Coping With Public Tragedy*, edited by Marcia Lattanzi-Licht and Ken Doka. Copyright © 2003, published by Brunner-Routledge.

From "The Role of School Counselors With Bereaved Teenagers: With and Without Peer Support Groups," by Ross E. Gray, in *The School Counselor.* Copyright © 1988, published by American Counseling Association.

From "Signs of Complicated Grief," in *Understanding Human Behavior in Health and Illness* (3rd ed.), by R. C. Simons. Copyright © 1985, published by Williams & Wilkins.

From "Warning Signs of Suicide," in *Some Facts About Suicide and Depression.* Copyright © 2002, published by the American Association of Suicidology.

Introduction

For many years, I have had a vision that there would be support available wherever there were teens whose lives were touched by loss and tragedy. Now, as I attend workshops at national conferences, talk with others serving this unique population, and look through books and videos, I am hopeful.

Grass-roots efforts to guide grieving children and teens are emerging from many concerned people. Parents, teachers, nurses, counselors, coaches, and spiritual guides are seeking appropriate and practical ways of accompanying grieving children and teens as they journey through the isolation, the turmoil, and ever-changing life experiences after a loved one dies. Educators, practitioners, and researchers are collaborating, sharing from their respective disciplines. It has become apparent that these young people can actually grow through the experience of grief, especially when they receive support and guidance from caring adults.

THE BEGINNING OF A VISION

This vision for me began almost 20 years ago when many of the families in our local hospice included a teen. When someone from the hospice team visited the homes, the teens would often be hovering in the shadows, seemingly wondering why these strangers were invading the privacy of their home at a most precarious time. When the parent died we considered whether these teens might be willing to join with other teens to wrestle with their grief in a group setting.

Since materials for helping grieving teens were scarce, the facilitators relied on the stories of the teens themselves to determine what themes were most important to their healing journey. Each group was different; each teen's grief was unique. We devised a variety of ways of approaching the topics, and learned what worked and what didn't. Both teens and facilitators grew in wisdom. I had gathered that wisdom into the first edition of *Helping Teens Work Through Grief*.

THE FIRST EDITION

The first edition included multidimensional activities, reflecting the many issues that touch the lives of grieving teens. It has been a practical resource manual, providing nuts-and-bolts information for caring adults as they take the steps toward establishing a grief group. Facilitators have been encouraged to listen to the teens and to trust their own inner sense in determining how to approach each unique group of teens. I have been told by many facilitators that *Helping Teens Work Through Grief* has been a valuable support in their work.

Yet, as images of toppling twin towers, rampages in high schools, and military troops heading off to foreign shores dominate the front pages of our newspapers, nationally and throughout the world, the loss of any sense of safety is becoming universal. The resulting fear, anger, and frustration often compound the turmoil of those already grieving a personal loss.

THE SECOND EDITION

In the second edition of *Helping Teens Work Through Grief,* I have touched on the topic of trauma, and how those whose lives are shattered by its effects need special care and evaluation before joining a teen grief group. More and more classes and workshops on the topic of trauma are becoming available to professionals to better serve those experiencing a more complicated grief.

The recent emphasis in the grief literature on "continuing bonds" has been encouraging. As Dennis Klass, one of the editors of the book by that name, said in conversation, "What took us so long?" In years gone by, there had been such emphasis on detaching from the person who had died in order to move through grief in a healthy manner. However, ongoing research has shown that children and teens do stay connected after their loved one has died. Rather than deterring their ability to move through their grief, their ongoing relationship seems to help their healing. In this edition, activities are provided to enhance the relationship between the teen and the deceased in order to help the teens successfully move on to a fuller life.

I have become increasingly aware of how spiritual questions of meaning and purpose are intertwined in the grief journey of teens. Teens can be encouraged to draw upon their spiritual resources at the time of great need. They can also be encouraged to wrestle with the incongruities that so often arise. Facilitators can find some practical ways of approaching these issues in chapter 13, "Moving On and Beyond: The Search for Meaning."

THE VISION

Unlike the geometric theorem, "The whole is equal to the sum of its parts," my experience with this dream of mine is that, indeed, "The sum of the parts is greater than the whole"—the whole picture of many people accompanying our youth through this life crisis and enabling them to live fuller lives because of their experience. As we facilitators continue to trust our own healing gifts and share with each other from our areas of expertise, we can together provide the much-needed support for grieving teens to embrace the challenge of growing through their grief.

I am especially grateful to those who have generously shared their gifts for this second edition:

Brittany O'Steen, who helped with the mechanics from the literary search to the final bibliography, and for her ongoing affirming presence.

Ellen Lindenbaum and Roy Hatch from Mercy Medical Center's McGlannan Health Sciences Library, for locating and sending the many articles from the literary search in a timely fashion.

My husband, Jim, my son, Sean, and Seon-Ho Choi, for their availability and practical help in walking me through the maze of computer technology.

My daughter Margaret and my supportive friends, Ann Shaw and Gloria Wessel, who were so willing to proofread parts of the manuscript.

Kathy Allen and Mary Richardson, who not only proofread, and generously shared their creativity through the activities "Fishbowl: Visualizing Grief" and "Sand Jacket: Experiencing Grief," respectively, but also offered ongoing encouragement.

My sister-in-law, Kathleen Kelly, who created the illustrations and shared her inspirational story of grief and art.

Kim Kinnett, who shared her artistic talents in her "Feelings of Grief" chart.

Nan Flynn, Fran King, and Amy Lieberman for their willingness to share ideas and materials and engage in conversation about how we might best live out our vision of serving grieving teens.

And particularly to former editors Jim Morgan and Joe Hollis, who believed in this project from the beginning, and my current editor Emily Epstein Loeb, from Taylor & Francis Group, who has been the guiding force for this second edition, from proposal to completion.

PART A
UNDERSTANDING GRIEVING TEENS
AND HOW TO SUPPORT THEM

Chapter 1

TEENS AND THE GRIEVING PROCESS

Being a teenager is about the struggle between dependence and independence. It's about the desire to abandon childhood patterns while feeling frightened by the consequences of adult behaviors. It's about sorting out a tangle of physical, emotional, moral and social changes. It's about deciding, "What do I want for my life?"

But life for the teen-in-grief is even more complex. The emotional turmoil of grieving can be unnerving for even the most secure teen. Intense and frightening mood swings make some question their sanity. (Perschy & Barker, 1990, p. 42)

TEEN YEARS:
THUNDERSTORMS AND TIGHTROPES

The adolescent years resemble a storm. The changing hormones rage, just like the wild winds of a summer thunderstorm. Like the thunder roaring and the lightning flashing, teen years are filled with outbursts of anger and frustration. A lull may follow. A pause, a taste of equilibrium, may precede the next wave of change.

Sometimes there are rainbows. Yes, adolescence is also a time of excitement as teens discover new strengths. They push their bodies to new limits in favorite sports. They stretch their minds by arguing every point in discussions. They further explore the many aspects of relationships. They question family beliefs in search of new meaning in their lives.

Each change brings an element of newness, and may also bring the pain of loss. However, teens sometimes experience the losses without the immediate benefit of the gains. This resembles a trapeze artist who has let go of one bar, hoping the other will be in place. These times can be filled with both exhilaration and hesitation.

When the bar is in place, the caution of anticipation changes quickly to elation. When the bar is not yet in the right place or contact is not made, then teens tumble into the safety net. This temporary setback is both frustrating and embarrassing. Worse yet, when the net is torn, or is not there, isolation, discouragement, and despair can overwhelm them.

Teens' issues might include:

Am I really cool?
Do I want to get sexually involved with my boyfriend?
Will I get into my first-choice college?
How can I tell Dad that I wrecked the family car?
My friend is threatening to commit suicide. Whom shall I tell?
My mom embarrasses me when she drinks.
I failed the test miserably.
Terrorists are attacking our country. Teens are shooting their peers. Is there any place
  that is safe?

These struggles alternate with highs:

I scored the winning points for the basketball team.
I made the cheerleading squad.
He invited me to the prom!
I got the scholarship.
I can hardly wait till the rock concert.
I passed my driver's test.

"Remember, the goal of adolescence is to become free of parental influence," my friend Elaine reminds me. The same son who insisted that a parent be present at every Little League game a few years ago now may refuse to walk through the mall with that parent, fearing that she may embarrass him by talking too loudly. After ignoring her presence, he may hand her a sweatshirt and shorts and then expect her to pay for them. Anthony E. Wolf (1991) described this ambivalence humorously in his book *Get Out of My Life, but First Could You Drive Me and Cheryl to the Mall: A Parent's Guide to the New Teenager.*

Recall the safety net. Teen thinking may go something like this: "I want to walk the tightrope alone. However, if I lose my balance, I might need you. I don't want to ask you to stand by, but recognize that I might need you to. Please don't fuss if I fall. I'm already too embarrassed about messing up."

The adolescent moves from simplicity to sophistication, dependence to independence, or better yet, interdependence, forming a set of beliefs and values that will determine the identity of this new person. It is a time filled with challenge, excitement, and success, interspersed with awkwardness and defeat, moving through this all-important passage to adulthood.

In spite of their ambivalent, and at times unpleasant behavior, an important task of adults who surround them is to help teens achieve a balanced and steady growth.

THE PROCESS OF GRIEF

There are various definitions of grief, mourning, and bereavement. According to Charles Corr, a leading educator in this area:

> *Grief* signifies one's reaction, both internally and externally, to the impact of loss.
>
> *Mourning* indicates the processes of coping with loss and grief.
>
> *Bereavement* identifies the objective situation of individuals who have experienced a loss of some person or thing that they valued (Corr, Nabe, & Corr, 2000, pp. 213, 220, 212).

There are many models of mourning; two specifically apply to teens. J. William Worden (1996) studied children, ages 6 to 17, and determined four tasks that children participate in as they move through the pain of their grief. Alan Wolfelt (2001a) observed some similar patterns as he has counseled many teens over the years and named some additional components to his model of the mourning process.

Tasks of Mourning

Worden's perspective on mourning is based on "attachment theory" as developed by John Bowlby. According to Bowlby, attachment theory "is a way of conceptualizing the propensity of human beings to make strong affectional bonds to particular others and of explaining the many forms of emotional distress and personality disturbance, including anxiety, anger, depression, and emotional detachment, to which unwilling separation and loss give rise" (Bowlby, 1978, p. 5). Teens may be helped to understand this theory at a couple of levels. First, ask them to recall times when they themselves were young, or some young person they observed, had wandered off and couldn't find a parent or guardian. Explore how that sense of being lost or abandoned triggers strong feelings of panic, fear, frustration, and possibly anger and terror, to name a few. Second, help them recognize that when someone they love dies, it is normal to experience a wide range of feelings, emotionally as well as physically, as they grieve. It is like a part of them has been torn away. The theories of Worden and Wolfelt elaborate on the specifics of this grief.

J. William Worden named specific *tasks* a child needs to accomplish in order to accommodate the flooding of these emotions and grow through the experience. The word "task" implies that the mourner needs to take action and participate in making the necessary adaptations to the loss. This action is described as "grief work." For leaders of a grief group, a knowledge of these tasks can provide a framework for planning appropriate activities.

In *Children and Grief*, Worden lists the tasks of mourning:

To accept the reality of the loss.

To experience the pain of grief.

To adjust to an environment in which the deceased is missing.

To emotionally relocate the deceased and move on with life (Worden, 1996, pp. 13–16).

To Accept the Reality of the Loss. Teens describe their disbelief when the phone rings and they think their parent is calling from a business trip, when in reality that parent has died a few weeks before. The human mind cannot comprehend the loss all at once and may temporarily shut down in a state of shock and numbness. "The physical and emotional memory I carry of the months following the death is one of floating in a cloud of gray gauze: alone, desolate, but fully cushioned from pain" (Browning, 2002, p. 465). In the early stages of the mourning process, this numbness is normal. If it lingers for many years, the denial would hinder progress through the mourning process.

Traditional rituals, as well as conversations about how the person died, can facilitate the movement toward acknowledging the reality of the loss.

To Work Through the Pain of Grief. The pain of grief touches many aspects of a person's being. Worden used the German word *schmerz*, which "includes the literal physical pain that many people experience and the emotional and behavioral pain associated with loss" (Worden, 2002, p. 30).

Hogan and Greenfield synthesized the studies of grief reactions of teens: "sleep disturbance, poor concentration, doing things alone, guilt, feelings of powerlessness and helplessness, restlessness, not being liked by peers, fear of dying, being sick more often, increased fears, depression, phobias, anger, nightmares, decreased sense of self-worth and suicidal thoughts, feeling uncomfortable when happy, difficulty concentrating, feeling responsible for the death, feeling overprotected by parents, anger at God, increased grief symptoms during family holidays, and believing their parents will never get over the death" (Hogan & Greenfield, 1991, p. 99).

Although some mourners are fortunate enough to find people who are able to support them as they work through the many feelings of grief, many people are encouraged to stop feeling sorry for themselves and get on with their lives. "To work through and complete grief means to face our feelings openly and honestly, to express or release our feelings fully, and to tolerate and accept our feelings for however long it takes for the wound to heal" (Tatelbaum, 1980, p. 9).

To Adjust to an Environment in Which the Deceased Is Missing. Worden presents three areas of adjustment a person needs to make upon the death of a loved one: external, internal, and spiritual.

External. There are some very practical tasks that need to be performed in families with children and teens. The death of a mother may result in more daily changes, such as, who will cook the meals, do the laundry, clean the house, and drive the car pools? The death of a father may mean that a bereaved mother may need to find work to support the family, while single parenting.

Internal. When a parent or someone very close to a teen dies, it often affects how the teen perceives himself or herself. Who could replace the listening parent, the one who made the teen feel special? Who can provide the safety net as the teen wrestles with the normal developmental tasks of adolescence? As bereaved teens ask "Who am I?" and "What do I want to become?" who will accompany them on this important part of their life journey?

Spiritual Adjustments. The death of a loved one can disrupt a survivor's sense of the world. This is particularly challenging for teens as they are searching for meaning in life. The death of someone close is often a catalyst for challenging existing beliefs. There are no "pat" answers to many of the profound questions that arise. This questioning may lead to a deeper spiritual understanding or it may lead to a sense of disillusionment.

To Emotionally Relocate the Deceased and Move on With Life. In earlier times, mourners were encouraged to detach from the person who has died in order to grieve in a healthy manner. However, more recently there is evidence that mourners often naturally find ways to develop "continuing bonds" with the deceased and are able to effectively move trough the pain of their grief. Studies show that grieving children stay connected by reviving memories of their parent. Often they are able to recognize that their parent is in a different form, from a different world. "The deceased now plays roles in the bereaved lives . . . protector, helper, supporter or confidante" (Normand, Silverman, & Nickman, 1996, p. 99). The child or teen "carries an awareness of and seems to act upon the deceased's beliefs, values, wishes, style, physiognomy, interests, and personality. She has made them her own and recognizes these as gifts from the deceased, as well as a link to him or her" (Normand et al., 1996, p. 109).

When teens reach important milestones or celebrate rites of passage in their lives, these can be times of intense emotion. A daughter talks of missing her mom as she shops for her prom dress. A son may feel let down at graduation as he sees other dads excited over their sons' accomplishments. Yet, they can continue to accommodate the loss.

Words may not adequately describe what actually takes place in the heart of the bereaved. The love the survivor had for the person who died can become transformed. It is still present, but carried in a unique way. Life may have renewed meaning and purpose. As a young woman wrote to her mother from college, "There are other people to be loved, and it doesn't mean that I love Dad less" (Worden, 2002, p. 37).

Wolfelt's Model of Mourning for Teens

Alan Wolfelt, having listened intently to the stories and the needs of teens, presented a slightly different model of mourning, specifically for teens:

> To acknowledge the reality of the death.
> To move toward the pain of the loss.
> Remember the person who died.
> Develop a new self-identity.
> Search for meaning.
> Let others help you now and always (Wolfelt, 2001a, pp. 4–9).

Wolfelt's model includes the same first and second tasks as in Worden's tasks. The aspects of new self-identity and search for meaning are touched upon in Worden's third task. To remember the person who died is similar to Worden's fourth task.

What is unique about Wolfelt's model of mourning is the special emphasis he places on the necessity for teens to *let others help them now and always*. He has recognized that teens may not want to "need" adults at the same time when they are striving for their independence. In Wolfelt's words to teens, "it's natural to want adults to keep out of your face." However, he further advises teens to talk to adults who care about them. "Or hang out with them without talking." Then he adds, "Talk to your friend instead. Join a support group. E-mail your thoughts and feelings to someone you don't have to look at every day" (Wolfelt, 2001b, p. 9). This important aspect of healthy grieving is further developed in chapter 3, "Social Support."

THE GRIEVING TEEN

Life for the teen in grief is complex. Affected by the developmental issues of adolescence, along with the emotional turmoil of grief, these teens face many unique challenges. The research of Fleming and Adolph (1986) on what happens to the ego development of the adolescent named five "core issues." Four of the five of the "core issues" were addressed in the Harvard Child Bereavement Study (Worden, 1996, p. 90).

> *The predictability of events*: When compared with their nonbereaved peers, bereaved children and teens showed greater anxiety and fear than their nonbereaved peers (Worden, 1996, p. 90).
> *Mastery and control*: Worden's study showed that bereaved adolescents believed they had less control over what happened to them than their nonbereaved counterparts.
> *Development of the self-image*: Bereaved teens were more likely to believe that their conduct and school performance were not as good as their peers. However, they felt that they were more mature than their nonbereaved peers.
> *Belonging*: Bereaved teens had more social problems and were socially withdrawn.
> *Fairness and justice*: Teens will often complain in a grief group, "Life is unfair!" They look at their friends' intact families and compare them with the tremendous pain their family is experiencing. A teen whose sibling died noted: "It taught me—I don't want to say it this way but this is sort of what I mean—it taught me to expect bad things, so that I could protect myself from when they happen. It made me realize the things that could happen, that do happen to people. It happened to me you know" (Balk, 1981, p. 317).

Wolfelt addressed the unique aspects of teen grief throughout his writings. Many people assume that the teen is "grown up" and then make unreasonable expectations, expecting the teen to support a parent or younger siblings, often to the detriment of his or her own grief journey. People think that teens will find the support they need from other teens, which may or may not be the case, unless, of course, the peer from whom they seek support has also experienced a major loss.

The normal developmental tasks of adolescence definitely influence the grief after the death of a parent. Because teens are supposed to be pushing parents away as part of their normal development, there may be a sense of guilt and unfinished business when the person dies. Teens may need to spend a considerable amount of time talking about their relationship with the parent while still alive in order to reconcile some of their turmoil (Wolfelt, 1990b).

Yes, bereavement certainly does impact the growth and development of the teen. However, when teens are supported through this life crisis of grief, growth can occur. Throughout this manual there are ways of encouraging teens to do their "grief work," enter into the struggle, and even experience positive outcomes.

Positive Outcomes

Oltjenbruns found in her study, "Positive Outcomes of Adolescents' Experience With Grief" (Oltjenbruns, 1991), that 96% of the subjects identified at least one positive outcome of grief. As teens are negotiating the myriad dimensions of grief, often there are life-enhancing outcomes. This may put the whole experience in a better perspective at a later date, and better prepare the teens for other major loss experiences in their lives. "Positive Outcomes of Grief," in chapter 13, "Moving On and Beyond: The Search for Meaning," assists teens in exploring this topic.

Chapter 2

WHEN TEENS EXPERIENCE TRAUMA

> Hilary couldn't fall asleep in her own bed and started climbing into Ginny's. She was having bad dreams—a recurring nightmare from when she was very young about her house burning to the ground with the three of them trapped inside. Hilary had also taken to blaming herself for her dad's disappearance and was preoccupied with guilty thoughts.
>
> Losing a parent is hellish in any instance. Hilary had the added horror of seeing hers vanish, suddenly and surreally, on TV. . . . Hilary, watching TV along with the rest of her sixth-grade class, saw one of the endless replays of her father's office building collapsing in a heap. (Morse, 2002, p. 1)

Hilary and her mom, Ginny, were one of thousands of families affected by the horrors of 9/11/01. Rando described how the 9/11 attacks contain all six risk factors that make any death traumatic and stimulate *traumatic bereavement*. The attacks were sudden and there was much violence, mutilation, destruction, and loss of life. Preventability, randomness, multiple deaths, loss of a child (including adult children), and a mourner's personal encounter with death were present in the survivors' stories (Rando, 2003, p. 267). The horror of this day was heightened by the fact that *all* these factors were present.

Trauma literature tells us that when *even one* of these factors is present, the survivor often experiences *complicated mourning*. Teens may experience a complicated mourning as the result a very private death of a loved one. The death may be hidden in a shroud of shame or guilt, such as a suicide, or a death related to AIDS. A friend or family member may have been murdered, or may have experienced a fatal accident or a sudden fatal illness. A teen may be mourning more than one loss (Goldman, 1996, p. 8).

COMPLICATED MOURNING

When mourning is complicated, the mourner attempts to deny, repress, or avoid aspects of the loss, its pain (Rando, 2003, p. 272). Linda Goldman uses the concept of "a frozen block of time" when the "child [or teen] is not in touch with his or her feelings of grief, or those feelings are ambivalent and in conflict" (Goldman, 1996, p. 7).

When a teen is experiencing complicated mourning, he or she would profit from an individual intervention with a mental health professional to deal with the overlay of trauma, or, in Goldman's terms, support the "meltdown" of "the frozen block of time." The initial focus needs to be on the trauma. "Failure to intervene in the trauma, and to focus instead exclusively or primarily on the loss, can result in either a retraumatization of the mourner or the mourner's flight from treatment" (Rando, 2003, p. 271). A skilled clinician can guide the teen through the trauma dimension of the complicated grief, thus enabling him or her to experience the issues of loss, and move into a grief group.

The process underlying posttraumatic reactions is called the stress response syndrome (SRS). There are two forms. The *first form* of SRS begins with the denial or numbing phase. Then the individual is confronted with phases of intrusive repetitions of traumatic memory, thought, feeling, or behavior, which alternate repeatedly with the denial and numbing. This alternation enables the teen to reexperience aspects of the trauma and then to shut them out, until the teen has made the necessary adaptation and the distress of the trauma ends (Rando, 1996, p. 152).

IMPLICATIONS FOR GROUPS WITH TEENS AFFECTED BY TRAUMA

When a teen has experienced the traumatic death of a loved one, the screening process for attending a grief group is essential for the welfare of the teen. The facilitator needs to evaluate whether or not the teen has moved through the trauma sufficiently to profit from the grief group's emphasis on the loss aspect of the complicated mourning. In addition to completing the registration form, it would be important to interview the parent and/or the teen. It may just be a matter of postponing the teen's participation in the grief group until it can be truly beneficial.

If, however, a teen is seeing a mental health professional, the facilitator could request written permission from the parent and teen to have a conversation with the mental health professional about the advisability of the teen attending a grief group, while being treated for complicated mourning. This may be appropriate for the *second form* of complicated mourning. The "posttraumatic stress elements are interspersed with the mourning and intervention requires paying relatively more attention to them initially, but not overlooking those aspects of mourning that are available to be treated simultaneously" (Rando, 1996, p. 153). Such collaboration between the professional focusing on the trauma and the facilitator of a grief group could provide the teen with the benefits of releasing the trauma and with the support of peers in working through the grief aspect of *complicated mourning*.

What is most important is the support the teens receive from those around them, both adults and peers. Although many people do not know what to say, or how to help, the energy of a caring person listening attentively certainly helps the teen. The teen may feel very alone; however, the visible presence of another person along this extremely painful part of life's journey lets the teen know that he or she is valued. Although the teen may not be able to totally believe this, during the worst of the crisis the seeds of hope are being planted. Looking back, the teen will be able to draw on the realization that he or she was able to *survive* something so awful. The teen may eventually realize the areas of *growth*.

In the group setting, some facilitators have found that they need to allow more time for the teens to share their stories when the grief is complicated. Also, the teens may need to tell their stories more than once during the set of sessions.

As a facilitator, you may be in a position to guide others, as they seek to find some word to express their caring. In *Children Changed by Trauma: A Healing Guide*, Debra Alexander (1999) offered a few samples. The words need to resonate with the person saying them; some will fit better than others. Speak from your heart in a way that invites the teen to stay with the process that leads to healing:

> I'm sorry it happened.
>
> Hearts can hurt the same way a broken bone does. Hurting is part of the cure.
>
> Broken hearts do heal.
>
> It's normal to feel sad at a time like this. [*Sad* could be replaced with any feeling.]
>
> Feelings can be confusing to people who have been through what you have.
>
> I can see you feel very angry/sad/scared right now. How can I help? (Alexander, 1999, p. 7).

Once again, the "right" words are not as important as the caring presence of people willing to be there for the teen.

Additional Resources

Chapter 13, "Moving On and Beyond: The Search for Meaning," has more information and ideas on offering support. In "Resource Material," there is a section on "Books Specifically Related to Trauma," and also listings in the "Organizations" section.

Chapter 3

SOCIAL SUPPORT

FAMILY

Picture a family mobile, where each person has a separate space yet is delicately held in balance, to form a unit. The mobile is attached to the ceiling. Each person moves freely within a certain range. If a wind comes through, each part of the unit whirls around, as the unit spins. The whirlwind eventually moves toward some sense of equilibrium. Daily living is filled with "windy" times, stirring a range of emotions. Yet there are life events that completely change the makeup of the balance of living.

If one of the figures is cut down, that delicate balance is completely disturbed. The other figures flail around. The figures are no longer in alignment. The mobile is never the same. Yet the mobile accommodates.

After a family member dies, life is forever changed. Whether it be parent or child who is gone, each family member is thrown into a state of imbalance. There is often a desperate attempt to quickly find the balance, to put life back together again. "I want my life to get back to normal, soon," is a common yearning. Families soon realize that this attempt to find some sense of equilibrium takes longer than anyone ever dreamt. This prolonged journey of grief and mourning draws on the deepest strength of each family member and of the other people in their lives.

Teens grieve within the context of the grieving family and an interpersonal network. The vacuum created through the loss of a significant relationship affects each person in the family, often causing great distress. Therefore, those who need the most help may not receive it from those who would normally be support persons in their lives (Vachon & Stylianos, 1998).

Now that we have painted somewhat of a bleak picture about social support within a grieving family, there are some pockets of hope. In his work with the Child Bereavement Study, William Worden (1996) determined that family interventions could help the family grieve in a natural setting. The interventions emphasize communications, readjustment, problem solving, or a combination. These interventions enable "family to operate as a natural support system and as a possible barrier to poor adjustment to the loss" (Worden, 1996, p. 151).

The "natural setting" of family intervention may be ideal for some families; however, there are other structures that can also help family members.

PARENTS

In a study of teens who have had a sibling die, 69% said that family members helped them in their grief; 47% said that their mothers and fathers helped them accept that their feelings were normal about their sibling who died, and 22% claimed that next of kin, namely, brother, sister, aunt, grandmother, or grandfather, was helpful. Is there something unique in these families because each of the siblings had died from a prolonged illness? Was there a particular type of bonding in anticipation of the death that made the families in this study better able to support one another in their journey through grief (Hogan & DeSantis, 1994)?

In a study of teens who had one parent die, 34% of grieving teens reported that their surviving parent was "helpful," and 30% rated the parent as "not at all helpful." "Of those teens who found parents unhelpful, some reported wishing they had received more support, but others reported that they had been unable or *unwilling to accept support* that was offered" (Gray, 1988, p. 187).

Parents Who Are Helpful

In the midst of their own pain, some parents are able to provide an atmosphere that allows grieving teens to explore their intense feelings. The parent may share his or her own pain to a degree, yet recognize that continual displays of hysteria and helplessness in front of children of any age may intensify the fear and cut off communications. Crying can bond family members; however, there is a fine line as to when it might become counterproductive. A helpful grieving parent may seek and receive understanding and encouragement from other adults, and may even be seeing a mental health professional. The parent may explore additional support opportunities for the children and teens, be it other adult relatives or friends, support groups, or a mental health professional recognizing the parent's own limitations.

When Parental Support Is Difficult to Accept

Because teens have started working toward their own independence developmentally, they don't usually want to need adults (Wolfelt, 1990a, p. 34). Accepting support from a parent during this precarious time may be counter to developing their autonomy, an important step toward adult maturity. The teen may be unable to respond to the offers of support from a parent. The doors to communication may have been closed from the inside, the teen's side.

When a parent dies, some teens may be apprehensive about openly sharing their true feelings with the remaining parent for fear of upsetting that parent, who is now widowed.

It may be too difficult to see the utter weakness of that adult, who may have been a guiding light in earlier times. It is scary enough to watch one parent die, without being constantly reminded that the other parent is vulnerable. Such a thought may be paralyzing to a teen to even verbalize to anyone, much less to the surviving parent.

When a Parent Is Not Helpful

Other parents may not be able to open the communication door. Communication patterns may have been strained before the death. The stress and strain of grief may further alienate parent from teen. Some parents may not even realize the impact the death has on the teens.

The parent may be so consumed by the pain of grief that there is little emotional energy to deal with the grief of the children, whatever the ages may be. For some parents, their own diminished mental health before the loss is further compromised by grief.

Adjusting to the many changes in everyday living can be all-consuming. Single parenting and working is challenging for most anyone, and most particularly for one who is mourning. Secondary losses of income, housing, and local support persons contribute to the struggle of just surviving. It is like treading water.

Just as the airline flight attendant suggests that in an emergency an adult put on an oxygen mask before assisting someone who is dependent, the grieving parent needs to seek adequate nurturing in order to help the children and teens.

In Gray's study of grieving teens, he recommended strengthening the networks that are already in existence whenever possible. This could include parent–teen communication sessions, or exploring family relationship issues with teens in their grief groups. Teens also suggested the possibility of providing a parent group (Gray, 1988).

Provide a Parent Group Also

Whenever possible, hold a group for parents at the same time as the teens are meeting. Ideally, provide groups for younger children also. Two main objectives of the parent group would be:

1. Provide support for the parent(s), enabling them to reflect upon their grief experience and explore their own grief. As the parents tend to their own grief, they will better be able to help their children, regardless of age. Before the group ends, it is important to help parents evaluate whether or not they have sufficient personal support. If they do not have enough support, encourage the parents to consider seeing a mental health professional for the sake of themselves and their children.
2. Provide information in order to better understand the grieving process of children and teens. When family members are attending a weekly grief support group according to their age group, it promotes dialogue about some of the aspects of grief when family members return home. This structure allows for healing of the family as a whole and will better enable the healing of each individual.

Parent Sessions

The facilitator of the parent group needs to provide a delicate balance between supporting parents in their own grief journey and discussing ways of helping their teens. If the teen group, parent group, and even a children's group meet at the same time, the facilitators could gather before the sessions to finalize plans. Leaders could present a common theme for each of the meetings, even though the specific activities and ways of approaching that theme will be different for each group. The leader of the parent group could provide information for the parents about what is planned for the teen and children's group. Parents have been pleasantly surprised at the ease with which they are able to discuss the many dimensions of grief after the topic has been explored with the children and teens at age-appropriate levels.

Facilitators can encourage the parents to talk about their greatest concerns regarding their teens. The camaraderie of other parents of grieving teens can be so helpful as parents become resources for each other. Some parents may be encouraged to allow the teens to question their beliefs, and learn how to support the teens in their search. Others may need help in establishing the fine line of setting limits, yet offering compassion when a teen's behavior is questionable. Issues may include celebrating the holidays, declining grades, changes in their lives, dealing with stress, and the intensity of emotions of grief or when it is important to find a good mental health practitioner. Usually there is no lack of topics.

Other Models for Parent Support Groups

If it is not feasible to have a parent group meet at the same time the teens are meeting, then gather the parents the week before the teen group is scheduled to begin. Give the parents a chance to talk about some of the difficulties in connecting with their teens around issues of loss. Encourage them to talk of what has worked for them, and what hasn't worked. Prepare handouts on taking care of themselves, along with some basic information on offering support. Lists of possible topics and how to approach some of them may give the parent the confidence to approach the teen. Additional information can be found in chapter 2, "When Teens Experience Trauma," and in chapter 13, "Moving On and Beyond: The Search for Meaning."

Another gathering could be scheduled during the midpoint at a time different from the teen group and another at the end of the set of sessions.

Of course, confidentiality always must be maintained within the group, particularly if the leaders of the parent group are the same as the leaders of the teen group. When the concept of a parent group was first discussed in one group, a response was, "As long as *you* don't lead the group. My dad needs to learn some communications skills, but I don't want him to be able to figure out my complaints against him. Could you get other leaders?" Different facilitators would be ideal. However, it is possible for the same facilitators to guide both groups.

OTHER ADULTS

Some teens are fortunate enough to have a large network of support people. These may include teachers, counselors, school nurses, scout leaders, spiritual leaders, employers, coaches, and, for many, their peers. These people may have the necessary skills, as well as the concern and compassion, so the teen knows that he or she is not alone. Alan Wolfelt advised grieving teens, "Talk to adults who care about you. If you don't want to talk to them, at least let them talk to you. Or hang out with them without talking. Talk to your friends, instead. Join a support group. E-mail your thoughts and feelings to someone you don't have to look at every day" (Wolfelt, 2001b, p. 9).

LEADERS OF A GRIEF GROUP

Adults who will be facilitating support groups for grieving teens need to be chosen with care. Consideration of the characteristics and skills of an effective leader may be beneficial. A rationale is provided for having coleaders to provide a meaningful experience for the teens.

Characteristics

"Adolescents are neither children nor adults. They seem to straddle both worlds and feel secure in neither" (Corr & McNeil, 1986, in Kandt, 1994, p. 10).

The key to success in working with teens is to have facilitators who like to work with and be with teens. They need to appreciate the intensity of the struggle and provide steadiness as teens wrestle with the chaos of grief. Teens are able to sense when adults are genuinely interested in their concerns or whether they are just putting in time.

Leaders need to provide a nonthreatening, safe atmosphere in order to earn the trust of struggling teens. Someone who is able to listen in an empathetic manner will enable teens to talk out and sort through the many issues competing for their attention.

Because the concerns of each group vary, the leaders will need to be flexible in planning and willing to allow the group to unfold. The group guidance model is different from a teaching model. Although there is some imparting of information regarding various aspects of grief, a primary focus is creating an atmosphere conducive for teens talking about what is most important to them. Leaders, therefore, need to be self-assured enough to tentatively plan a session yet allow it to take a very different course.

Finally, leaders need to be comfortable with issues of death and grief. There are appropriate times when leaders can demonstrate that they have dealt with grief issues in their own lives and acknowledge their own personal growth from these experiences. This self-disclosure can help clarify an abstract concept and help teens know that others actually have grown through their experiences of grief. Yet it needs to be done sparingly and in a way where the teens will not feel overwhelmed by the facilitator's description of his or her own grief.

Guideline for Choosing Facilitators

Asking two simple questions can help determine what is important in choosing a facilitator:

1. If I were hurting, what characteristics would a person need to have in order for me to trust that person with the story of my pain?
2. If I had a secret, what would I look for in someone I would share it with?

Whether these questions elicit a list or a felt sense, they will provide a "knowing" that will likely lead to a good choice.

Skills

Facilitators need group dynamics training to promote interaction within the group and thus enable each person to speak comfortably. The art of facilitating a group effectively takes time to develop. One of the leaders could have some past group experience while another is learning.

Because there is a teaching or guidance component to a grief group, leaders need to be able to present information in a clear, concise manner. Leaders need to have a good sense of timing, knowing when to teach and when to listen and support the expression of the struggle.

Why Have Coleaders?

It is wise to have *two* persons leading a group. If there are male and female participants, it is ideal to have one male and one female facilitator.

When group members are exploring their grief, many subtle expressions are occurring simultaneously. One facilitator can be monitoring the activity of the group, while another is offering support to a particular teen. Sometimes a bereaved teen may express something that triggers some unexpected reaction within one leader. Sensing that, the other leader may need to take over the discussion, temporarily allowing the other leader to refocus.

Two persons bring different styles that can serve the group members better. Some teens may connect with one leader, while others may relate better to another leader. It is important, however, that the leaders be collaborative. If misunderstandings arise, it is essential that both leaders be willing and able to work out their differences *outside* the group time.

From a practical perspective, if one leader suddenly comes down with the flu or some other emergency arises, the meeting still can be held. Unnecessary cancellations can be disruptive to the participants. The teens depend on this all-important continuity.

It is recommended that one of the leaders be a mental health professional. If this is not possible, it is essential that there is a professional with whom the leaders consult with between each meeting. This professional can assist the leaders with group process, can advise about particular issues needing expert opinion, and can help determine when individual professional help for a particular teen might be warranted.

Peer Review

When there are groups meeting simultaneously involving children, teens, and parents from the same families, it is important to gather after the session to process what has been happening in the groups. This provides an opportunity to discuss how best to help the group members, how to modify the process, and to plan for the next meeting. When something has been triggered within a facilitator, this is a valuable opportunity to receive the support of peers, allowing time and space to process what is happening. This sense of "team" adds a spirit of cohesiveness to the whole program.

PART B
THE TEEN GRIEF GROUP

Chapter 4

THE VALUE OF A GROUP IN DEALING WITH GRIEF

"I thought my feelings were dumb and was ashamed of them. Then I came to this group and realized that others have the same feelings. When I am with others outside this group, I feel abnormal. Here I feel more secure. I am a normal grieving person." Laurie, age 15 (Perschy, 1989, p. 3)

PEERS: SOME ARE HELPFUL; OTHERS ARE NOT SO HELPFUL

When teens are in the throes of developing their autonomy, they distance themselves from their parents. They seek acceptance and respect from their *peers*. Yet when they are grieving the loss of a loved one, there is a mixed review as to the helpfulness of their friends. Some are very helpful; others are not.

According to Gray's study, some grieving teens appreciated those peers who treated them normally, as they just wanted to be included in activities as usual. Close friends provided emotional support. However, "a larger network of peers seemed to withdraw from the bereaved person, leaving the bereaved teen feeling socially isolated and abnormal" (Gray, 1988, p. 187). Some of these teens just don't know what to say or do; others are dealing with their own anxieties about death (Vachon, Lyall, Rogers, Freedman-Letofsky, & Freeman, 1980).

NORMALIZING THE EXPERIENCE OF GRIEF

Seventy-six percent of teens who participated in a grief support group "were more likely to report that they felt peers understood them after their loss than did other bereaved teenagers" (Gray, 1988, p. 188). There is a unique bond that forms when peers gather for a common purpose, even peers who initially did not know one another. This has been shown again and again when bereaved teens have had the courage to join a group to explore their grief experiences. "Many believed that they were only understood or were only able to really express their grief when they met other students who were going through the same difficulties" (Gray, 1988, p. 192).

A teen grief group provides a valuable opportunity to enable the members to normalize their experience. Their unique common bond helps to create an atmosphere that allows them to share their vulnerability, and therefore grow through their grief experience.

A *safe place* to express the craziness of grief, the uncomfortableness of mood swings, the embarrassment of crying in public, the inability to concentrate, is what a teen-in-grief seeks. Teens have expressed the importance of being "understood, cared for and loved." They believed that it was helpful to their grieving process if "they were part of a network of people who allowed them to grieve on their own terms and timetable and to disclose powerful thoughts and feelings about their grief without sanctions or attempts to discount the depth of their feelings" (Cobb, 1976).

The teens in the group serve as valuable *resource persons* for one another. As they share their stories of loss, they know that they are not alone. They provide practical hints of how to deal with the many changes in their lives. They learn how to break down problems into manageable parts and give and receive support for trying new behaviors.

Chapter 5

INITIATING AND ORGANIZING A GRIEF GROUP

INITIATING THE PLAN

Teachers, guidance counselors, or coaches may become aware of a few teens who have experienced a significant loss. The adults may consider gathering them together to provide tangible support. The school system would be a logical place, whether within a particular school or within a cluster of schools. Churches, synagogues, or mosques where teens are affiliated may have enough members at one time to warrant a teen grief group. Hospice bereavement departments, individual mental health professionals, and funeral-home personnel have formed such groups.

What Type of Group?

Group guidance is an effective model for teen grief. The group leaders present some general information about grief and its impact on the lives of the bereaved. When needed, they provide activities with themes that touch on the issues they sense are affecting the teens. The structured activities provide an opportunity that fosters reflection and discussion around a great variety of themes. After a couple of sessions, the teens can be encouraged to gradually assume leadership roles in determining how the later sessions unfold.

Goals and Objectives

Goals and objectives help the facilitators focus on what is important. Specific objectives can be revised as leaders interact with a particular group of grieving teens. It is important to modify the approach, balancing the particular needs of each person with the general needs of the group.

Goals

To provide a safe, supportive atmosphere for teens as they explore the many facets of grief after a loved one dies.

To promote the teens' active involvement in the process of mourning, making it a learning experience and a catalyst for growth.

Objectives

To provide appropriate information about the process of grief and how it affects one's life.

To encourage teens to talk about and express their fears, anger, regrets, sadness, desires, and concerns, if they are willing.

To encourage teens to explore with other group members, as well as the leaders, any particular grief-related issues touching their lives.

To help teens address pertinent aspects of grief, either spontaneously or through specific structured activities.

To assist teens in examining their current support system and discuss how to expand it, if needed. This expansion may include finding a mental health professional for ongoing support.

PUBLICIZING THE GROUP

Early publicity across a broad spectrum of places where teens gather will help determine whether or not enough participants will register. It takes a while for the information about the group to filter through networks in order to reach the maximum number of bereaved teens.

Create a Press Release to Fit Your Group

The wording of the press release (Figure 5.1) is significant. The term "support group" may seem threatening to some teens. When we discussed how to reach other teens at the end of one of our groups, one teen told us, "When you call it a support group, it sounds like you expect us to come and spill our guts to a bunch of strangers." They suggested that in the publicity we describe the group as a learning experience about grief and list issues related to grief. Add a statement that the teens will determine additional themes.

ISSUES OF GRIEF
(for teens)

When teens experience the death of someone close, they often feel isolated, confused, sad, and angry. They speak of feeling out of sync with their peers and cannot concentrate on their schoolwork. [Your organization] is sponsoring a six-session series on *Issues of Grief* for teens who have experienced the death of a relative or friend.

Topics will include the following:

Grief: What is it and how does it feel?

Dealing with difficulties in concentrating.

Coping with changes.

Taking care of yourself.

Commemorating a special life.

Other topics proposed by the participants.

This program begins [insert date, time, and place].

For more information, and to register, call [insert phone number].

Figure 5.1   Sample press release.

Create a Brochure

Design a flier that captures the essence of your group. Enclose a few copies with the press release, to be distributed to interested individuals. Text for a sample brochure is provided in Figure 5.2. This brochure is designed to be folded in thirds and personalized by the sponsoring organization.

TEEN GRIEF GROUP—Sponsored by [Your Organization]

Why Come to a Teen Grief Group?

To learn about the grief: What is it? How does it feel? What helps you learn from the experience, and grow through it?

To meet other grieving teens with similar issues, concerns, adjustments.

To learn to relax, gain energy, release bottled up feelings, and thus move toward a better balance in life.

- - - Fold - - -

Who Is Invited?

Any teen, ages 12 to 19, who has had someone close die, be it parent, grandparent, sibling, other relative, or friend.

Any teen who is tired of feeling isolated by the pain of loss.

Any teen who is coping with changes as a result of the death of a loved one.

- - - Fold - - -

What Do We Do?

Talk about how the feelings of grief affect our lives and how we can work through some of the pain.

Listen to others speak of memories about the person who died, and add your own memories, if you wish.

Talk about problem areas such as declining grades, reactions of friends, dealing with anger, moodiness, crying, and any other topic that is important to you.

Eat, drink, and socialize.

Figure 5.2, page 1.   Sample for 8.5″ × 11″ brochure, to be folded in thirds.

Issues Discussed in Former Groups

- declining grades
- meddling relatives
- preparing for the holidays

- putting fun things back into my life
- expanding my support system
- looking for the answer to "why?" questions

How to Care for Myself While Feeling . . .

- sad
- lonely

- confused
- guilty

- angry
- fearful

- depressed
- frustrated

- - - Fold - - -

Address [of sponsoring organization]

```
┌─────────────────────────────┐
│                             │
│        Address label        │
│                             │
└─────────────────────────────┘
```

- - - Fold - - -

TEEN GRIEF GROUP

"I thought my feelings were dumb and was ashamed of them. Then I came to this group and realized that others have the same feelings. When I am with others outside this group, I feel abnormal. Here I feel more secure. I am a normal grieving person."

Laurie, 15

Figure 5.2, page 2.   Sample for 8.5″ × 11″ brochure, to be folded in thirds.

REGISTRATION AND INTERVIEW

Prepare a Registration Form

Decide what information is both essential and helpful for you as leaders to know before the group begins. Eventually, a roster list with addresses and phone numbers may be compiled and distributed to the group members. Include that request for permission on the form. A sample registration form is provided in Figure 5.3.

Send the Registration Form to Parent or Guardian

When a parent, guidance counselor, or other adult advocate calls about a particular teen, send a registration form to be completed by the parent or guardian. Attach to the registration form a copy of "Signs of Complicated Grief." (Find copy in Appendix A.) Send a cover letter specifying times, place, directions, names of leaders, fees, if appropriate, and any other necessary information. Ask that the form be returned two weeks before the first meeting to allow time for the leaders to peruse the forms and talk with the teen, when needed. This is essential when the person who died experienced a traumatic death.

Call the Teen Before the First Meeting

After the parent or guardian has sent in the paperwork, it helps to bridge the gap for the teen to receive a call from one of the facilitators. The leader can explain how the group runs, touch on what topics will be discussed, and offer to answer any questions about the group. The leader should explain the rule of confidentiality to reassure the teen.

This initial phone call may alleviate the anxiety the teen may experience when anticipating being with a bunch of strangers. The teen now has connected with at least one person who will be in the group. The leader also can assess whether or not this group is appropriate for this particular teen. For instance, one teen told the leader that he didn't want to come, that his mom was "making" him come. The facilitator suggested that he try it for a week or two. The teen said that he absolutely would not say a word during all six weeks. Since the teen was so adamant, it was clear that he would not be an appropriate group member at this time.

Often there is resistance to come to a group, but usually the teens are willing to give it a try. Once they bond with the other teens, they continue to come, and appreciate the experience.

TEEN GRIEF GROUP—Registration Form

Teen's Name _____ Date of birth _____ Age ____

Parent/Guardian's Name _____

Street Address _____ City, State, Zip _____

School _____ Year in school ____ Phone _____ Work phone _____

In case of emergency, if parent/guardian is not reachable, list someone you would like us

to contact. Name _____ Phone _____

May we include your teen's name, phone number, and address on the roster list that will

be given to the other group members? Y _____ N _____

Name of person who died _____ Date of death _____

Relationship to teen _____ Cause of death _____

Sibling(s) name(s) and age(s) _____

_____

What other significant changes have taken place in your teen's life during the past two years?

_____

What other experiences has your teen had with someone who has died? _____

_____

It is imperative that a teen who is exhibiting behaviors which may be harmful to him
or herself or others be seen by a mental health professional before joining a grief group.
The therapist will help determine when it would be appropriate for a teen to attend such
a group. At that point, it may be advisable for the teen to attend the teen group while continuing to meet with the therapist. Does your teen exhibit any such behaviors?

Y _____ N _____ Please comment. _____

_____

Attached to this form is a description of "Signs of Complicated Grief." As you read
the descriptions in relation to your teen, are there signs of complicated grief?

Y _____ N _____ Please comment. _____

_____

Are there other concerns for your teen you wish to comment on? _____

_____

Parent/Guardian Signature _____ Date _____
Please continue explanations on the back of this sheet.

_____

Figure 5.3 Sample registration form.

Chapter 6

GROUP DESIGN

Length of a Typical Session

A typical session is 75 to 90 minutes long. An additional 15 minutes allows the flexibility for teens to finish speaking, rather than cut off the sharing to have a punctual ending. This leeway ought to be explained to parents.

Closed Group or Ongoing Group

Some agencies provide an ongoing group, allowing teens to join the group when they feel they are ready. They can also determine when they have received what they needed from the group and are ready to leave the group. The group is always available for them.

Other groups have a beginning date and an ending date. There is an effort to foster the formation of bonds early in the group experience. Anyone who wishes to join the group after the second meeting is encouraged to wait for the next group to begin.

Number of Meetings

For a closed group, although it is ideal to schedule an 8-week group, teens are often only willing to commit to 6 weeks. The group members may wish to continue meeting beyond the agreed-on length of time, or a reunion group may be scheduled. Some teens come back for a second set of sessions, or return as peer facilitators. There is some repetition; however, the leaders usually vary the plans enough to accommodate the needs of each group and its members.

Number of Activities per Meeting

Facilitators could plan two or three activities, depending on the number of participants and their willingness to talk. It may be advisable to overplan, particularly if the teens in that particular group are reticent to talk. If the teens are particularly talkative, some parts can be rescheduled for the following week, or simply dropped. It is of the utmost importance that immediate concerns of the teens take priority over any scheduled agenda.

Choosing the Space

An open space with comfortable chairs would be an ideal setting for a teen group. However, other structures will work. Some meetings require a table with chairs allowing enough elbow room to do an art project. Some teens prefer to continually meet around tables, giving them easy access to snacks. Gathering in a circle of chairs or even on a carpet would facilitate some other activities. The outdoors on a pleasant day might be the perfect setting for the initial icebreakers or the closing affirmation activity.

THE FIRST TWO MEETINGS

The first two meetings set the tone for the remaining sessions. Often, the teens are nervous and avoid eye contact. While some are withdrawn, others may talk nonstop. Facilitators need to be settled rather than be scurrying about with last-minute preparations. The welcoming, nonjudgmental attitude of the leaders helps to reduce the tension.

Facilitators might consider having common games available like tic tac toe, blockhead, or art supplies to make a personalized name tag or card, while waiting for the rest of the teens to arrive. The activity around pouring drinks and obtaining snacks provides a nonverbal connectedness and increases the comfort level.

Introductions

It is so important to allow time for the teens to get to know one another. Chapter 7, "Helping Teens Connect," offers a selection of ways to bond with each other, which is essential for the teens to feel safe enough to share.

Confidentiality

Rules and clear boundaries create the safety necessary for self-disclosure. Therefore, it is essential to establish the ground rule of confidentiality at the beginning of the meeting. Self-conscious teens are cautious about sharing private information if they feel it would be made public or misused. If the group members agree that a personal story stays within the confines of their meeting room, teens may speak more openly about important issues.

However, confidentiality does not prevent teens from talking about general information regarding grief, or their own personal insights—for example, "Now I better understand why my grades have dropped. A lot of grieving people have a hard time concentrating." It is *not* all right to mention personal content that someone else shares. For example, "See that girl over there in the bleachers? She is in a group with me, and was really upset at our last meeting. Her brother died of AIDS." Group members expect confidentiality to be honored.

The concept of confidentiality may be difficult to totally comprehend during the first explanation. At various times throughout the meetings a leader may further differentiate between what is okay and what is not okay, by using examples from that particular session; for example, "It is all right to share that a lot of grieving teens are angry at meddling relatives, overprotective parents, or incompetent doctors. It is not okay to say, 'Sylvia, who is in my teen group, ran away from home because she was angry at her dad who is way too strict.'"

There are some gray areas. The teens themselves could be brought into the discussion of what they would expect to be kept confidential and what is all right to share. When in doubt, encourage teens to ask the group members and arrive at a consensus.

Value of Working in a Group

A facilitator could begin a discussion about the value of a group, including:

1. Grief groups can reduce the isolation of bereaved teens.
2. Being with other teens provides a chance to share ideas of how to deal with similar situations, feelings, and issues.
3. Leaders have background and experience about the grieving process, and how to promote healing and growth while moving through grief.

Why Did You Come?

Sometime during the first session, the facilitator may ask, "Why did each of you come to the group?" It may help to give a few responses of what other teens have said during their first session, such as to learn more about grief and the mourning process, to talk with others who are grieving, and, most commonly, because my parent made me come.

Often a parent, who may be recently widowed or grieving the death of a child, may not know what to do to help the teen. The parent simply insists that the teen attend the group. The teens laugh when they realize that there are others who are being "forced" to be there. They can be reassured that those who have come before them to other groups in retrospect were very glad that they did come.

Housekeeping Information

Provide specific information about the place, time, and frequency of meeting, as well as inclement weather plans, absentee notification, and transportation issues. This will help prevent confusion later.

Ground Rules

1. Each person is encouraged to speak, but no one will be coerced to do so. Members of the group may just say, "I pass."
2. Each person is expected to listen to the person who is speaking and refrain from criticizing another. A member may add something, but needs to be accepting of what others share.
3. Physical violence is totally unacceptable.

Descriptions of Grief

Grief is the normal process that occurs after a person has experienced the loss of a loved one. This group focuses on loss as a result of death. Acknowledging the pain of grief and learning ways to deal with it lead to healing and growth.

"The Process of Grief" in chapter 1 has some valuable information to elaborate on the process of grief. More specific activities are listed in chapter 10, "Learning About Grief."

Telling Their Stories

It is important for the teens to be able to talk about the death of their loved ones in order to make the death real. There are questions in activity 7.6, "Telling One's Story," to assist the teen in focusing on various aspects of the death. Sometimes hearing someone else talk about the loss of a loved one can make it easier to tell one's own story. If there is any hesitancy in the group about going first, the leader, or peer facilitator, who has experienced the death of a loved one, may begin.

The teens could be gently nudged into telling their story, yet not be put on the spot. Remember, even if someone chooses not to speak, that person may still benefit from listening to others tell their story. There is a certain connectedness in knowing that another person their age has experienced a loss, even if the details are different. This connectedness can often be seen in the faces of the listeners, or in the nodding of the heads. There is that sense of "I am not alone." However, it is important to the other group members that, at least, the teen who has chosen to "pass" be willing to say who died, and whether it was sudden or not.

THE MIDDLE MEETINGS

During the first two or even three meetings the leaders will have gleaned some information about what important issues need to be addressed. This will influence the planning for the meetings that follow.

The "Specific Structured Activities" in Part C of this book include many diverse practical plans to help teens focus on issues relating to their grief. Plan one meeting at a time. What comes up spontaneously is more important to focus on than a preplanned program. During each meeting, be attentive to issues and feelings that could be addressed during the next meeting. A spirit of flexibility will ensure that the teens will claim the group as their own and will therefore participate enthusiastically.

THE FINAL MEETING: SAYING GOODBYE AND EVALUATING

Importance of Closure

"Do we have to stop?" whispered a shy 13-year-old girl. "I wish this group could go on and on." Others agreed, saying the group was very important to them in their struggle with loss, and they didn't want to lose *it*, too. Often strong bonds develop in a relatively short period of time. Therefore, leaders should prepare the group for closure gently, but clearly. The teens need an opportunity to say good-bye.

Saying Goodbye to the Group Members

There is often pain in the goodbye, yet acknowledging that pain enables people to move on. Teens could be encouraged to write notes to each of the other group members. As an ending activity, tape a paper plate on each person's back. Have everyone write on each other's plate something positive about that person. As they finish moving around the room, have them remove the plate and read what others have written about them. Talk about how it feels to give and receive positive messages. This type of activity helps the teens to deal with the loss of the group. If a roster of names and phone numbers has not been previously distributed, this would be a good opportunity to have it available, having asked permission from a parent or guardian ahead of time.

Obtaining Feedback From Participants

During the last session, allow time for the group members to evaluate what was helpful and not so helpful in the group. They could then say what they will miss and what they will take with them from this grief group.

Evaluating the group's activities reinforces the reality that the group is ending, and provides helpful information for the leaders as they plan for future groups. A sample "Evaluation" form is given next.

Evaluation

An evaluation is a helpful way of finding out what was helpful and what was not helpful. The sample in Figure 6.1 is customized to what actually took place in that particular group. It is simple to devise and gives some clear feedback. Some programs, however, may need a standard evaluation in order to do statistical measurements of the effectiveness of a program. Facilitators will need to check before the last session with their own sponsoring organization to determine if there are any specific expectations from the evaluative process.

Peer Facilitators

When the next group begins, some teens from former groups may be invited to become peer facilitators. This allows them to assume some leadership within the group and still participate as a member. These peer helpers can make new members feel welcome, lead "getting to know you" exercises, and assist with facilitating the discussions by going first.

BEYOND THE GROUP

Encourage teens to stay connected through their phone list. Close bonds may have formed in the group, and the roster may be the avenue to nurture these relationships for those who wish.

Facilitators can decide if they have the time and energy and willingness to be committed to a follow-up program. It is better that the teens not be told of any follow-up program unless it is a priority for the facilitators. Teens do not need one more disappointment.

However, some ideas that have worked are:

Phone calls—3 or 6 months after the group ends.
Reunion—1 month after the group ends.
Camp or retreat in the early summer.

These experiences give the teens another opportunity to connect, and give the facilitators a chance to get a sense of how the teens are doing.

EVALUATION

Please help us plan for future groups by circling the number that best describes how helpful each of these was for you.

1—not very helpful
2—not helpful
3—okay
4—helpful
5—very helpful
N/A—not applicable

Grief Art Project depicting grief	1	2	3	4	5	N/A

Stories:

Tear Soup	1	2	3	4	5	N/A
Sadie Listens	1	2	3	4	5	N/A
The Precious Present	1	2	3	4	5	N/A
Writing to the person who died	1	2	3	4	5	N/A
Writing how you think the person would respond	1	2	3	4	5	N/A
Expressing feelings through clay	1	2	3	4	5	N/A
Determining how music affects our feelings	1	2	3	4	5	N/A
Learning about nutrition and exercise	1	2	3	4	5	N/A
Talking about supports in my life	1	2	3	4	5	N/A
Using Affirmations	1	2	3	4	5	N/A
Yoga & breathing exercises	1	2	3	4	5	N/A
Stresses in our lives	1	2	3	4	5	N/A
Positive outcomes of grief	1	2	3	4	5	N/A
In general, how was the group	1	2	3	4	5	N/A

Thank you for having the courage to come.

Figure 6.1   Sample evaluation.

PART C
SPECIFIC STRUCTURED ACTIVITIES

Ideally, the teens gather and begin to share the pain of their own stories of grief. Gradually, they learn to listen attentively to the tales of the other teens, offer an encouraging word, or share an insight. Although this ideal group dynamic sometimes occurs, it is not the norm.

In reality, teens come together, not knowing one another, not sure what the group is all about, and often not even wanting to be there in the first place. A well-meaning or concerned parent, who is grieving the loss of the same person, just wants to make sure the teen will be all right, so that parent may insist that the teen attend the group.

The icebreakers provide the opportunity for these nervous teens to interact in an informal and even a fun way. The tension usually lessens, and the teens are more ready to enter into the group experience.

When the teens begin to share their stories about how their loved one died, changes in their daily living, or whether school personnel are helpful or not helpful, the up-tight bodies continue to relax. They become aware that *they are not alone*. They are normal grieving teens.

Structured, More or Less

Many factors contribute to when this sharing takes place: the number of reticent versus outgoing teens, the range of ages, or simply the chemistry of the group members. If the sharing is difficult, the facilitators may choose more of the structured activities. However, when the group gels easily, the conversations around pertinent topics of grieving occur more spontaneously. Regardless of what has been planned, the teens' own spontaneous discussion of issues related to grief always takes priority. The agenda prepared by the leaders is secondary to the immediate needs of the teens.

Don't be overly concerned about participants who seldom speak during the sessions. Experts assure us that even the silent members of the group can benefit from being there. The group experience gives them the chance to reflect on their own process and learn by listening to the others. However, if you sense the teen is distressed by what is shared, it might be helpful to recheck the registration form to see if there are signs of trauma. If a teen becomes more withdrawn, a conversation with the parent about additional mental health services might be necessary.

As leaders, you may decide to use part of one activity and connect it with an idea of your own or with something that evolves in the group. Someone may want to share a newly written poem, or one that he or she found. A magazine article, drawing, or song may resonate with the experiences of your specific group.

The enthusiasm will grow as the teens begin to invest in the planning and assume the leadership for topics that touch on the essence of their concerns. The facilitators will then truly personify Webster's definition of facilitate: "to make easier or less difficult." The creative space the adults have fostered allows the teens to heal. Teens then recognize that as difficult as this process of grief is, they can continue to draw on their inner strength and their giftedness and, with the support of others, can move through life's most challenging experiences. Hope begins to take on a new meaning.

Chapter 7

HELPING TEENS CONNECT

It is so important to begin the first, and possibly the second, session with activities that will help the teens get to know one another. Facilitators may use an icebreaker from their own repertoire or choose from those described in this chapter. These nonintrusive icebreakers foster trust among the participants, which is so necessary for them to share their very personal experiences of the many facets of grief.

This time helps the teens relax. Often they have ambivalent feelings about joining such a group. Talking about things they like to do is a very gradual entry into the group.

7.1. *Getting to Know You* moves the teens into a circle throwing a beanbag, while sharing on "safe topics," like food, music, color, and sports. It is a fun way for teens to introduce themselves; even shy teens join right in. Teens can then think of their own themes, and sometimes they are willing to continue leading the group in the warmup activity.

7.2. *My Coat of Arms* is another form of introducing teens, this time using drawings. This may appeal to those who learn through tactile involvement. The drawings from the six spaces can move the teens to a deeper sharing.

7.3. *Line Up* and 7.4. *Stress Busters* help to energize the teens as they move throughout the room, exploring the likes and dislikes of each other. The spirit of the group members lightens.

7.5. *Mirroring* introduces in a casual setting the wide range of feelings of grief, from difficult to pleasant. It is also an opportunity for the facilitator to intersperse information about feelings, such as, "Any feeling could be considered a feeling of grief, not just the obvious ones of sadness, guilt, or anger," or "Each person's grief is unique, although there may be some common threads among many people."

7.6. *Telling One's Story* is an important activity to include during the first session after an icebreaker or two. Telling how their loved one died and how they responded to the death helps the teens connect on a deeper level. It normalizes the experience of loss, recognizing that each person there is grieving the death of someone close. They are no longer with others who cannot comprehend the extent of the feelings of grief. They are with other young people who are able to relate to each other's pain.

Activity 7.1 GETTING TO KNOW YOU

Goal

To help teens connect with other group members.

Objectives

To get to know some information about the other group members.

To model that it is all right to do enjoyable things, even while grieving.

Procedure

Form a circle. Throw a beanbag, a light beach ball, or a small pillow around the circle. As each person catches it, have this person say his or her name. Continue with any of the ideas from the following list. Add other categories (15 to 20 minutes). This activity may be used for another session by presenting new categories. Ask the teens to come up with other categories.

Name
School
Grade
Favorite activity
Least favorite activity
Favorite holiday
Favorite food
Least favorite food
Favorite music group
Favorite color
Favorite sport (active or spectator)
If I won $100, I would . . .
If I won $1,000, I would . . .
If I could travel anywhere, I would go to . . . with . . .

Activity 7.2   MY COAT OF ARMS

Goal

To introduce the group members to each another.

Objectives

To assist the teens in sharing information about themselves with the group.

To elicit information for the leaders to plan the agenda for future sessions.

Procedure

1. Make 8.5″ × 11″ copies of the instructions and the blank shield (Activity Sheet 7.2) and distribute to each person to complete.

2. Have the teens choose a partner and talk about their coat of arms.

3. Return to the larger group. The teens could talk about their own coat of arms, *or,* the partner could introduce the person to the group by telling about the other person's symbols. If the partner introduces the person, allow time for the person to add to the introduction anything else about him- or herself.

4. If any of the symbols elicit further discussion, allow it to continue. (30 to 40 minutes)

MY COAT OF ARMS

Draw:

Symbol of one thing you like to do.

Symbol representing a goal you accomplished in the last 3 years.

Symbol that reminds you of the person who died.

Symbol representing the worst thing about grief.

Words or symbol. What made you come to the group?

Symbol of one change you have experienced since your loved one died. (30 minutes)

Activity Sheet 7.2   Coat of Arms. Permission is given to photocopy for grief group use. Source: Drawn by Kathleen Kelly. Used with permission.

Activity 7.3   LINE UP

Goal

To help teens feel more comfortable with each other.

Objectives

To help teens get to know something about one another.

To actively participate in a fun way.

Procedure

Place a line on the floor using tape or a string. Designate one side of the line as "I agree" and the other side of the line as "I do not agree." Have the teens stand up and explain that you are going to read a list of statements. If they agree, then they move to the "I agree" side of the line. If they don't agree or would answer "no" to the statement, then they should move to the "I do not agree" side. Read the statements one by one with ample time in between for people to move and see where others stand. (15 minutes)

It is fun to go to the beach on a sunny day.
It is okay to go to the beach on a rainy day.
Looking at the stars is relaxing.
Journaling helps me clear my head.
The school day should be shorter.
The school system should change to year-round school.
Skydiving is a healthy sport.
Winter sports are scary.
Scary movies are adventurous.
Scary movies keep me awake at night.
Lasagna is a favorite food of mine.
Ice cream isn't all that it is cracked up to be.
It is a personal decision whether or not to keep a cluttered room.
It is all right to cry in public.
Life has been a lot more confusing since I am grieving.
Life isn't fair.
Growth can come from a painful situation.
There are people in my life who understand my grief.
I know what to do with my anger.
I have a sense that the person who died is still connected with me.
I came here because someone insisted that I come.

Activity 7.4   STRESS BUSTERS

Goal

To help teens feel more comfortable with each other.

Objectives

To help teens get to know something about one another.

To expand the number of practical ideas for dealing with stress.

Procedure

1. Talk about stress and how it can interfere with our peace and happiness. Make copies of the list of ways of relieving stress in the boxes on the bottom half of this page. Distribute half page to teens.
2. Encourage the teens to find someone who participates in an activity in one of the boxes. Ask that person to sign his or her name in the box.
3. At the end of a specific time, ask the teens to come back to the group. Discuss what they learned about the others in the group, and what other stress busters work for them. (15 minutes)

Stress Busters

Exercises	Sleeps	Reads a good book	Dances or ice skates
Listens to music	Writes in a journal or diary	Takes a walk	Enjoys being outdoors
Sings or plays an instrument	Works on a craft or a hobby	Meditates	Plays with pets
Participates in winter sports	Participates in water sports	Enjoys cooking or baking	Does deep breathing exercises

Activity Sheet 7.4   Stress Busters. Permission is given to photocopy for grief group use.

Activity 7.5   MIRRORING

Goal

To connect with other group members.

Objectives

To explain the connection between feelings and how our bodies may express them.
To connect in a fun way with another group member.

Procedure

1. Recall with the teens that they may have played "Simon Says" and "Copycat" games over the years. Explain that "mirroring" is an adaptation that will help them identify the variety of feelings connected with grieving.

2. Have each person choose a partner whom they do not know well. Ask one person from each pair to pantomime the expression of a feeling of grief (i.e., anger, guilt, sadness, helplessness). Add others. Have the partner copy the movement.

3. Have everyone look around at how others expressed the feeling movement.

4. Make comments about the connection between feelings and how our bodies express them. Although this activity may seem like an artificial expression of feelings, highlight the more subtle real-life connectedness, such as sick stomach, headaches, and so on.

5. Have the teens vary the degree of intensity of the feeling. (i.e., express very angry; then express annoyed). Encourage them to notice the differences. Comment on how an emotion can easily escalate when under stress.

6. Continue to mirror various feelings. If they are ready, have a teen lead the activity using some of the feeling words below.

7. Begin to discuss how we can deal with difficult feelings in a healthy way. Additional specific ideas are provided in chapter 11, "Moving Through the Pain." (10 to 15 minutes)

Feelings of Grief (Partial List)

afraid	disgusted	lonely
angry	enthusiastic	peaceful
ashamed	excited	powerless
confused	frustrated	sad
dejected	guilty	stressed
depressed	hurt	worried
desperate	inadequate	

Activity 7.6   TELLING ONE'S STORY
(Important Activity for First Meeting)

Goal

To make the death of a loved one more of a reality.

Objectives

To encourage teens to focus on the circumstances of the death of their loved one and how it has affected them.

To provide an opportunity to reflect upon and share about any memorial services which may have taken place.

Introductory Comments

After a person dies, it is very important for the bereaved person to talk about the many dimensions of the experience. The more a person tells the details of how their loved one died, and details about the burial, and how the person may have responded, the more real the death becomes.

As teens tell their stories, parts of another person's story may connect with their own, whereas another part may be different. The teens begin to observe that there may be common threads about grief, yet each person's grief is unique. They are being exposed to the wide range of emotions that fit under the category of "grief." Often, the teens have spoken about not feeling so alone. There are others who seem to understand what they are experiencing.

Procedure

1. Make copies of "Telling One's Story." Fold the copies hiding Part B temporarily. This allows the group to focus on one topic at a time. Distribute the copies.

2. Using Part A, concentrate on the story of the loved one's death and the teens' immediate response. Encourage the teens to jot down notes in response to the questions if they wish.

3. Invite the teens to share their stories. If there is any hesitation, a peer facilitator or a leader could briefly share a personal experience of grief. This can provide a model for sharing.

4. If there is time, move on to Part B to focus on the memorializing of the loved one. However, you may decide to wait until the following session.

5. Optional: Follow up by highlighting through conversation or by listing on poster board the many feelings of grief. This list could be used at a later meeting.

7.6 TELLING ONE'S STORY (Teen Copy)

These questions may be helpful in recalling events around the death of your loved one. If it helps, jot down notes.

Part A

Who died? How did he or she die?

Was it a short or long time ago?

How did you find out that your loved one died? Who told you?

What was your immediate reaction after hearing of the death?

Did you see your loved one after the death?

How do you feel now?

Part B

What was it like for you to see (or not see) your loved one? Was there a funeral, shiva, or other kind of memorial?

Were you involved in the service?

What parts were really difficult?

What parts were okay?

What memory of the person who has died makes you feel good?

Activity Sheet 7.6   Telling One's Story. Permission is granted to photocopy for grief group use.

Chapter 8

TEENS CARING FOR THEMSELVES

As teens wrestle with the wide range of intense feelings, they can become so enmeshed in their grief that they may not recognize that they can actually focus on taking care of themselves. Their thinking may be clouded and their self-esteem may be low. They may be asking, "Do I deserve special treatment?"

Therefore, the teens may need to be encouraged to consciously choose to take care of themselves. It will help to provide a balance, so essential in order to deal with everyday living. This is not a small feat while feeling consumed by conflicting emotions, so often characteristic of grief.

There is an element of choice as to how anyone moves through their grief. Teens may need to be convinced that by making conscious decisions to care for themselves during this difficult part of their life journey, they can actually assist with some of the healing of their pain.

The activities in this chapter fall under the theme of self-care. The facilitators of a grief group can offer a range of opportunities in this area.

8.1 *Clearing a Space* is a way of reminding the teens, "You are not your grief." This simple exercise can help the teen to temporarily put aside some of the painful dimensions of grief. They can use it when they feel overwhelmed, or each evening before they fall asleep, as a way of tapping into the core of themselves that is basically okay.

8.2 *Affirmations* helps to reinforce what we are learning about grief. It is a form of "self-talk." With continued practice, this tool can help teens put their grief in perspective. Affirmations could be added to any session to reinforce important learnings. There are additional affirmations in Appendix I. Facilitators or teens can develop their own.

There are two parts to 8.3 *The Precious Present*. The first part focuses on living in the moment. It can help the grieving person to recognize and honor the feelings of grief. It can also help the teen to recognize that there are pleasant moments in everyday life. The handout, entitled *The Present*, is a unique way of allowing the teen to appreciate some of the valuable aspects of themselves at a time when they tend to underappreciate their accomplishments.

8.4 *Supports in My Life* is a structured activity to identify the teen's concern, "Who will be there for me?" Facilitators can remind the teens that they are not alone. If, indeed, some teens do not have enough support in their lives, the topic "Who else could I add to my support system" can be explored.

8.5 *Words That Help; Words That Don't* helps teens realize why they feel uncomfortable when certain people say certain things. They need to decide whether or not it is worth "re-educating" certain people. They can choose who can actually be supportive.

Activity 8.1   CLEARING A SPACE

Goal

To introduce the teen to a practical way of creating a peaceful space, temporarily freeing the grieving teen from some of the pressure of difficult issues and feelings.

Objectives

To assist teens in naming some issues and feelings that are causing them difficulty.

To present a simple way of providing respite from these concerns and to experience some fresh energy.

Introductory Comments

This Chinese proverb can empower teens to modify some of the intensity in their lives.

> "You cannot prevent the birds of sorrow
> from flying over your head,
> but you can prevent them
> from building nests in your hair."

Sometimes we may feel like the birds have landed on our heads, and are beginning the construction of a nest or two. Grieving persons need a break from their sorrow.

Procedure

1. Make a poster of the words of the Chinese proverb. Have the group members discuss its meaning in relation to the mourning process. Talk about some things they already do to "prevent them from building nests in your hair." Explain how this imagery is one way of "taking a break" from their grief.

2. Guide the teens in the imagery on the next page.

3. Include the following in the discussion:

   Ask the teens how the experience was for them. What part was helpful? What was difficult?

   Remind the teens that they can return to one or more of the issues or feelings they had put away at another time. Right now, they can just enjoy the space they have created.

Explain that when they do the imagery themselves, they would not need to put their hand on their knee. It was only necessary in a group setting.

Ask the teens about times when it would be helpful to use this imagery. (30 minutes)

Clearing a Space

Close your eyes. Notice your breathing for a few moments. (Pause.) Allow your imagination to move around inside, and notice where you feel tight, uncomfortable, or all right.

Ask yourself, "Is there anything in my life right now keeping me from feeling really good?" If anything comes, put your hand on your right knee so I know when to continue.

(When everyone, or almost everyone, has their hand on their right knee, continue.) See if you can set that whole thing aside, by putting it on an imaginary shelf, in a box, behind a tree, or any image that moves it away from you. If it resists, tell it that you need some space, just for now. When you have been able to set it aside, put your hand on your left knee to let me know you are finished. While you are waiting for the next step, enjoy the space you have created for yourself.

Repeat the previous paragraph two more times.

Spend some time enjoying the space you have created. (It may not be totally stress free. However, there may be some fresh energy.)

Before you open your eyes, remind yourself that you can create a space for yourself (Campbell & McMahon, 1991, pp. 7–8).

Activity 8.2   AFFIRMATIONS

Goal

To show teens how to encourage themselves through positive statements.

Objectives

To help teens recognize that they can influence how they feel by thinking and repeating positive statements.

To introduce affirmations and how to use them to provide a better balance.

Introductory Comments

There are many aspects of grief that are painful and draining. They need to be honored some of the time. However, it is also important to provide a balance by repeating and visualizing positive, energizing thoughts. The word *affirm* means to assert positively.

In time of crisis if I tell myself that I cannot possibly handle this, I will be reinforcing the sense of helplessness I am feeling. On the other hand, I can say something like, "I am feeling helpless at this moment; however, I have felt this way before and I got through it just fine."

Procedure

1. Choose some affirmations from the Affirmations section in Appendix I. Type them in large letters. Cut them, so that each teen may choose one that fits. Display them.

2. Talk with the teens about trying to provide a balance and how the teens are capable of actively helping themselves by changing some of their self-defeating thoughts to more positive ones.

3. Discuss some of the negative thoughts people have while mourning, and how the teens might retool them into affirmations. It is important that the affirmation makes sense to the person using that particular one.

4. Have each teen choose one he or she created and draw it in large letters, or have them choose one from the displayed ones. Spend a few minutes with the teens, encouraging them to reflect on the affirmation. See if an image arises that matches the thought. Have them slowly repeat it over and over again. If a symbol comes, suggest that the teens draw it on his or her sheet.

5. Ask teens where is the best place to post their sheet. Where else could they write it? What are other ways they can remember to say the affirmation during the coming week?

6. At the next meeting ask what worked and what didn't work.

Activity 8.3   THE PRECIOUS PRESENT

Goal

To help the teen reflect on and share about living in the present.

Objectives

To guide the teens in reflecting and sharing about living in the present through a story.

To help the teens recognize special things about themselves through a graphic of a present.

Introductory Comments

The many losses connected with grief often pull grieving people toward the past. Because the pain is often so great, it is difficult being in the present or even considering the future. These two activities center around the theme of living in the present. Facilitators may decide to use one or both of them in the same session.

Procedure

Part A

1. Read the book *The Precious Present* by Spencer Johnson to the group, asking the teens to jot down anything in the story that makes sense to them or anything that bothers them.

2. Ask the teens to share anything they liked or didn't like from the story.

3. Display posters with some of these additional quotes and open to discussion.

   "I can choose the precious present whenever I want."
   "The precious present is something precious I can give to and receive from myself. For I am precious" (Johnson, 1984, pp. 56 and 64).

4. Encourage the teens to honor the struggle they are experiencing, taking time to reflect on their feelings, and yet be open to the next moment, to experience that fully, too. (25 minutes)

Part B

1. Make copies of "The Present." Distribute to the teens and ask them to fill in the four quadrants.

2. Talk about the various ways we respect ourselves while we are grieving and how they are reflected in each of these statements, honoring pastimes, accomplishments, feelings, and oneself by allowing others to be supportive of us.

3. Ask them to share what they wrote.

4. Encourage the teens to place "The Present" in an obvious place in their rooms to remind them of the "precious present." (20 minutes)

Activity 8.3 THE PRESENT

Some of my favorite
pastimes are:

I am proud of:

I can set a goal,
and meet it.

I could try:

When I am angry, sad,
depressed or frustrated,
it helps me to:

When I need to talk,
these people are
helpful:

I could also try:

If I need to talk,
I could also contact:

CRISIS HOTLINE:
OTHER ADULTS:

Activity Sheet 8.3 The Present. Permission is granted to photocopy for grief group use.
Source: Drawn by Kathleen Kelly. Used with permission.

Activity 8.4   SUPPORTS IN MY LIFE

Goal

To provide a structure to help teens examine their support system and determine whether or not they need to add other people to it.

Objectives

To encourage teens to identify what persons are supportive of them and what interests and activities are meaningful to them.

To help teens decide if there are times when they may need more support, such as a professional counselor, and how to find one.

Introductory Comments

It is important for teens to have an opportunity to examine the supports in their lives to make sure that they have a satisfactory network to do their "grief work." Such a network includes the persons in their lives who care about them and support them in good times and in difficult times. In return, the teens can recognize that they are support persons for others. Our pets, activities, and belongings, along with our network of people, can give meaning to our lives.

Procedure

1. Find the phone number of an emergency hotline, and add it to "Supports in My Life" worksheet. Distribute copies of the worksheet, talking briefly about the importance of support, and ask each teen to fill it in.

2. Through the discussion, guide the teens in identifying who is really there for them. Help them explore whether or not they have enough people in place during this difficult time. Explore with the teens how they could broaden their network if more support would be needed. Are there teachers, counselors, clergy, rabbis—people whom they trust, but haven't reached out to before? What important traits would the person need to embody: good listener, compassionate, and so on.

3. Talk about the services of mental health professionals, such as psychologists, counselors, and social workers, and how essential it is to meet regularly with someone when people are continually overwhelmed, depressed for long periods of time, or have frequent thoughts of suicide. Encourage teens to talk with their parent/guardian about checking who is available through their medical coverage. Talk about how the

first person they go to may not necessarily be the best fit, so they may need to meet with more than one person to find the right "match." Ask the teens to add their perspective, because many of them may have already been in therapy. Some may have had a good experience; others may not.

Although there is less stigma about seeing a professional than there was years ago, this is an opportunity to emphasize how valuable it can be, not just for now, but throughout their lives.

Point out the hotline phone number and explain that it is available 24/7. When they or their friends need immediate support, they can call. They can even call on behalf of another person to find out how to help that person in an emergency.

8.4   SUPPORTS IN MY LIFE (Teen Copy)

A healthy support system is important, especially while we are grieving. This list will help identify who is there for you and what things give you energy. Fill in the specifics.

People Who Care About Me

Friends:

Family:

Relatives:

Neighbors:

Teachers:

Counselor/mental health professional:

Minister/priest/rabbi:

Other adults:

Interests That Are Important to Me

School related:

Spiritual:

Work:

Sports:

Arts/music:

Other:

Things That Are Important to Me

Pets:

Memorabilia (pictures, special items):

People I Could Add to This List to Strengthen My Network

1.

2.

When a crisis occurs, and your support persons are not available, call the local hot-line number: (30 minutes)

Activity Sheet 8.4   Supports in My Life. Permission is granted to photocopy for grief group.

Activity 8.5   WORDS THAT HELP;
WORDS THAT DON'T HELP

Goal

To encourage teens to evaluate words people use in relating with them and how they might modify interactions that don't resonate well.

Objectives

To provide an opportunity for teens to discuss what people say to them that helps and what people say that doesn't help.

To support teens as they have "a conversation" with some of their closest friends in order to gain more support.

Introductory Comments

In an article about teens attending a grief group, entitled "Crazy Grief," the teens often complained about the thoughtless comments people made that were annoying, and even disturbing. Giving teens a chance to air their frustration may turn into a problem-solving activity of what they might do or say to those who were meaningful to them before their loss.

People just may not know what to say. Yet the teen may feel alienated because of what he or she perceives as a lack of sensitivity. Some of the teens may be willing to invest the time and energy to figuring out how to approach people who had been important to them and thus to regain some support for themselves.

Procedure

1. Facilitators could mention some comments that they know have bothered bereaved people, or use quotes from the article "Crazy Grief" (in Appendix E).

   Adult: "Aren't you over that yet? Didn't your dad die over a month ago?"
   Teacher: "It's been a month now. You ought to start working on your grades."
   Relative: "Now you are the man of the family" to a 14-year-old.
   Adult: "Take care of your mother." She wanted to shout, "What about me?"

2. Ask the teens about what people say that helps them, and what they say that doesn't help. They could even gather around two large sheets of poster board, labeled *Helps* and *Doesn't Help*, and write their comments.

3. After they have released some of their frustration, guide them toward making a third list: "What would you like people to say to you?" As the discussion continues, sometimes it becomes clear that there is no set of "right" responses. What one teen might like, another may not. However, there may be responses that everyone would appreciate.

4. Guide the teens even further by asking: "Are there people whom you know that really care about you, but may not know what to say in this situation? Is it possible to have a conversation with one or more of these persons, and talk about what helps and what doesn't?"

   This quote from "Crazy Grief" could illustrate how someone who is frustrated with how her friends are treating her and knows how she would like it to change. Karin says, "Some people treat me like I have a disease. They either totally ignore me or, if they do talk, they are afraid to mention the word 'death,' or the person's name. If someone would just say they heard my dad died, and did I want to talk, I would know they cared, yet wouldn't feel pressured to respond. What really helps is a hug from a friend."

   This discussion could move beyond words and could lead to a discussion of what can friends *do for* you, or *do with* you. Reassure the teens that it is all right to ask for what would be good for them, especially at a time like this.

5. Teens may want to role-play with one another in twos, practicing how they could initiate a conversation with friends on what helps and what doesn't through words or actions.

6. Encourage teens to choose an affirmation that applies for them to use during this coming week. (30 minutes)

Chapter 9

CREATING A JOURNAL

The middle-of-the-night darkness that often accompanies grief can be unyielding. Who is there to listen to the bizarre conglomerate of feelings? There may be a trusted friend who is willing to be awakened, to be with the grieving person. However, this willingness is often short-lived. Life must go on for most people.

"How can I be listened to?" a teen may be asking. A simple spiral notebook or an elaborate cloth-covered one can be a wonderful help in working through the craziness of grief. The blank page is always available, will not judge unfavorably, and allows the teen the freedom to say whatever comes to mind, day or night.

In journaling workshops, participants are encouraged to write as they would speak. They can even write in dialogue form with someone—living or dead—who has had a strong impact on their lives. It is a powerful way to recall the good times and the not-so-good times, and even to experience some resolution to conflicts or unfinished issues.

As they "talk" about their thoughts and experiences, the ongoing written dialogue can foster the "continuing bonds" with the person who has died. Elena Liser, MD, wrote in the introduction to *I Will Remember You: A Guidebook Through Grief for Teens*, "Grief is about finding a way not to move on past but to move along with who this person was to you" (Dower, 2001, p. xix). A journal can be just the right tool.

Unlike a diary, which records a pragmatic listing of events, journal keeping is a powerful asset in acknowledging, naming, expressing one's innermost thoughts and feelings, honoring them, and moving through them.

In her pamphlet "Write Grief," Gail Jacobsen encouraged grieving persons to write as a great way of organizing their thoughts.

> You will gain insights about your feelings, fears and concerns; the more you become aware of your thoughts and choices, the better your judgments will become as you reassemble your shattered life. Overwhelming concerns will become manageable, thoughts less fragmented. Healing will occur both from the writing and from the reflection upon the writing. (Jacobson, 1990, p. 5)

As Jacobsen struggled with her own grief, she confided that she desperately wanted to know *why* there was death, loss, and grief. Finding no suitable answers to the *why* questions, she turned her focus to answer *how* you grieve. She found that writing enfolded and transformed her grief.

A word of caution: If teens are experiencing the intense feelings over a long period of time, it is important that they talk with a trusted adult, and possibly a mental health professional. Teens could be cautioned, "Remember to monitor your own feelings. If your feelings are getting more and more intense, and you are feeling depression or despair, that is a red flag. Talk with someone about getting professional help."

9.1 *Structured and Customized Journal* and 9.2 *Structured and Customized Journal* provide a variety of approaches to journaling for those who are grieving. Journaling can be incorporated into any session.

CREATING A JOURNAL (Teen Copy)

A journal can be a wonderful tool for exploring our feelings of grief. In the middle of the night when no one else is around, the blank pages invite us to write as we would speak.

We can just "let it all hang out," pouring out the anger, frustration, guilt, or any of the other feelings of grief. We can write another letter back to ourselves, using words that we sense the person who died would say to us. We can write about the good times and the not-so-good times.

Remember, however, that if your feelings are getting more and more intense, without any relief, and you are feeling depressed or despairing, that is a red flag. Talk with a trusted adult and consider getting professional help. Learn what the crisis hotline phone number is, and use it when no one else is available.

Grief is a healing process. During the painful times reach out to someone. You don't need to move through this challenging part of your life journey alone.

Hotline phone #:

ACTIVITY 9.1   Structured and Customized Journal

Goal

To introduce teens to the benefits of writing as an effective tool in moving through grief.

Objectives

To enable teens to clarify what they are feeling and thinking through journaling.

To provide a concrete way of processing feelings.

Introductory Comments

Structured and customized journaling enables the teens to further explore a particular topic or theme through the written word, or by drawing. A piece of paper with a few open-ended sentences or statements or questions to reflect on, write about, and share with the group can provide an opening to a deeper understanding of some aspect of grief.

Ongoing

As facilitators become aware of particular themes and issues, they can develop additional journal sheets which can be used at later meetings.

Continuing After the Group Ends

At the end of the sessions, facilitators may provide additional pages to encourage further exploration of feelings of grief and commemoration of the person who has died. Teens can also be supported in journaling in an unstructured way (Activity 7.2) if that has not yet been done during the sessions.

Procedure

1. During the second or third session, distribute folders to the teens to collect the completed journal pages. Encourage the teens to decorate their folders, personalizing them.

2. When facilitators sense what themes would lend themselves to being explored more thoroughly through writing, they could prepare customized journal pages. There are

journaling sections in three separate chapters of this book, reflecting the theme of that chapter:

Chapter 11 Moving Through the Pain
Chapter 12 Continuing Bonds: Commemorating and Connecting with the Person
                Who Died
Chapter 13 Moving On and Beyond: The Search for Meaning

They can serve as a sample for developing other open-ended sentences and questions. Write or type the items on a sheet of paper, allowing space for writing a response.

3. Distribute the journal papers, allowing time for the teens to complete them. Some groups like to bring in their own background music; others may prefer the quiet.

4. Time provided for sharing after journaling is often rich and meaningful. Because of the privacy of the material, it is important to remind the teens that they are free to "pass" when the writing is too personal. Often special bonding occurs when the teens share from the heart with one another.

Activity 9.2　UNSTRUCTURED JOURNALING

Goal

To encourage teens to keep an ongoing journal to explore the many dimensions of their grief.

Objectives

To provide the materials to keep a journal.

To explore feelings, questions, issues, conflicts, solutions, as well as an ongoing relationship with the person who died.

Introductory Comments

1. Provide a simple notebook or folder for teens to use as a journal. Allow time for them to personalize the cover by decorating it.

2. Make copies of the "Creating a Journal (Teen Copy)" page. Distribute the copies for the teen to put in their notebook or folder.

3. Encourage teens to write in their journals when they feel they need to talk about the feelings of grief and there is no one available to listen. Just let the words flow onto the paper without concern or worry about punctuation or grammar, as though they were talking to a good friend. This can provide a record for the teen of how he or she is moving through the feelings of grief.

4. Share with the teens how journaling on a regular basis is a way of staying connected with the person who has died, although it may seem strange to the teens at first. Through a series of letters the teen can get a sense that the loved one is still available. The teen may begin by writing about what is important to him or her. Then the teen can try to get a sense of how his or her parent might respond. The dialogue can continue.

    On an anniversary, birthday, holiday, or other important day, encourage the teens to experiment with different writing forms, such as poetry, stories about the person's life, or phrases the person who has died used to use. They could even add some drawings to the writing, or add some words to a drawing.

5. Invite the teens to bring in and share their journal entries if they feel comfortable doing so.

Using a Commercially Developed Journal

Facilitators can learn more about journaling and preparing journal pages by looking at what is available commercially. There are many journals for grieving teens that provide the opportunity for an in-depth experience. If a particular teen may be drawn to journaling, one of these journals could extend the group experience of reflecting on important aspects of grieving. The section in the Resources entitled "Journals for Teens" includes many current titles.

Chapter 10

LEARNING ABOUT GRIEF

Teens are often relieved as they learn about a model of grieving. Whether the facilitator presents a formalized step-by-step explanation of Wolfelt or Worden, or a simple graphic of the "Feelings of Grief" as in Appendix C, teens are nodding when something resonates with how they feel or have felt. Even if a particular teen connects with only one or two of the feelings or behaviors, he or she soon realizes that what seemed like craziness is actually normal grief.

The activities in this chapter enable teens to reflect on the mourning process and gain some insight into their own experiences of grief. Choose the activities in relation to the needs and maturity of the teens in the group. There may be just one part of an activity that would fit a particular group's needs. At a later group session, another section may be appropriate.

Because 10.1 *Helps in Moving Through Your Grief* is so comprehensive, the facilitators may pick and choose what seems most needed for a particular group based on the initial sharing of their stories. Parts 1 and 2 may be used during an earlier session; parts 3 and 4 may be presented at a later time, or not at all, depending on other issues and choices that are more pertinent.

10.2 *Choosing to Work With Your Grief* could be introduced by saying something like this: "If you have ever seen someone swimming against the current, you know how much energy is entailed. However, swimming with the flow is a totally different experience. Just as in swimming, people can fight the process or choose to spend the time and energy to enter into it." This activity helps teens recognize that we can "choose" how to proceed.

Some individuals learn better through discussion, others through watching, and still others by being physically engaged in an activity. Activity sheets 10.3 and 10.4 employ a combination of styles of learning.

In 10.3 *Fishbowl: Visualizing Grief*, the fishbowl provides a visual representation of grief by adding drops of food coloring to a bowl of water. The teens are engaged by naming or describing the feelings. Drops of bleach are added to the murkiness as teens describe ways of coping with and moving through their feelings.

In 10.4 *Sand Jacket: Experiencing Grief*, the tangible dimension is in the form of one pound packages of colored sand. As the teens describe one of the feelings of grief, a package is attached to the jacket, symbolizing the heaviness of grief. When the teens offer one idea to cope with that feeling, a pound of sand is taken out. This experience makes grief so much more concrete.

Activity 10.1   HELPS IN MOVING THROUGH YOUR GRIEF

Goal

To provide information about the process of mourning and an opportunity to reflect on one's own experience of grief.

Objectives

To introduce information about working through grief, namely, the tasks of mourning as presented by William Worden (1996).

To help teens identify experiences as they connect with Worden's model of grief.

To suggest ways of continuing the movement through grief.

Introductory Comments

William Worden has provided a model to explain how persons accomplish particular tasks as they move through the difficult times and begin to feel more balanced. These are called the *tasks of mourning*.

To accept the reality of the loss—knowing the deceased person is no longer alive and will not physically be a part of their everyday lives.

To experience the pain of grief—experiencing a variety of intense feelings and working them through as a part of the grieving process.

To adjust to an environment in which the deceased is missing—struggling with the many changes as a result of the death, including the practical aspects of daily living and the effects upon the sense of self and perception of the world.

To emotionally relocate the deceased and move on with life—acknowledging the value of the relationship with the deceased, yet allowing oneself to get on with life (Worden, 1996).

To understand better the tasks of mourning, these activities help teens connect these concepts with their own experiences. The questions are structured to enable leaders and group members to come up with other appropriate ways to move through these various task.

"Feelings of Grief" (Appendix C) provides a graphic representation of some of what teens experience. This less verbal tool may be used in conjunction with the activity sheets, especially part 2, where teens are encouraged to create a group collage. Each group may choose different feelings.

"Grief Art Project," a large poster representing the feelings of grief in a cartoon-like form, has been a valuable catalyst for discussion. Information for ordering it can be found in the Resource section.

Procedure

1. Present an explanation of the tasks of mourning by William Worden to the whole group, using the background in the chapter "Teens and the Grieving Process." (15 to 20 minutes)

2. Explain that the tasks are not necessarily moved through consecutively. Someone who is grieving may be experiencing more than one task at the same time.

3. Provide charts with the definitions of grief, mourning, and bereavement and explain the difference:

Grief signifies one's reaction, both internally and externally, to the impact of the loss (Corr et al., 2000, p. 213).

Mourning indicates the processes of coping with loss and grief (Corr et al., 2000, p. 220).

Bereavement identifies the objective situation of individuals who have experienced a loss of some person or thing that they valued (Corr et al., 2000, p. 212).

Include in a discussion of the mourning process:

- Feelings are neutral, neither good nor bad. It is important to identify, own, and honor each of our feelings.

- The feelings of grief are a normal response to the loss of someone close to us.

- There are healthy ways to be with and direct our feelings.

- It is okay to cry. Tears can be a symbol that we have loved and are hurting inside.

- You do not need to grieve alone. It is important to let those around you know how they might be able to support you. It may also be useful to talk with others who were less connected or not connected at all with the person who has died, as long as they can be compassionate and nonjudgmental. A grief support group can provide a safe place to talk about your grief.

- There is no right or wrong way to grieve. It is your own process, done in your way and in your time.

Make copies of the appropriate Activity Sheet. Provide time for teens to share their responses. Because so much information is being presented, this activity could be split between two sessions. The leader could introduce the first and second tasks one week, and the third and fourth tasks the following week.

Activity 10.1   HELPS IN MOVING THROUGH YOUR GRIEF, Part 1 (Teen Copy)

William Worden worked with grieving persons. He observed what they experienced as they moved through the turmoil of their grief toward a place of healing. These experiences are called the *tasks of mourning*.

> *To accept the reality of the loss*—knowing the deceased person is no longer alive and will no longer be present physically.
>
> *To experience the pain of grief*—experiencing a variety of intense feelings and finding ways of coping with and moving through them.
>
> *To adjust to an environment in which the deceased is missing*—struggling with the many changes as a result of the death, including the practical aspects of daily living and the effects upon the sense of self and perception of the world.
>
> *To emotionally relocate the deceased and move on with life*—acknowledging the value of the relationship and continuing bonds with the deceased, yet allowing oneself to get on with life (Worden, 2002).

Task 1. In dealing with the first task of grief, *to accept the reality of the loss,* it may take a while to comprehend the reality of death. Describe when you found yourself:

• Listening for the footsteps of the person?

• Expecting the person to call?

• Hoping, and sometimes believing, that there was some mistake and the person was still alive?

Jot down any difficulty you had accepting the reality of your loved one's death. (Continue writing on the back of this sheet.)

It is painful to face the fact that the person will not return physically. However, by gently reminding yourself of the loss, it eventually will become more real.

(25 minutes)

Activity 10.1   HELPS IN MOVING THROUGH YOUR GRIEF,
Part 2 (Teen Copy)

Task 2. In dealing with the second task of grief, *to experience the pain of grief,* "I must be losing my mind," is a common complaint of the grieving teen. "The least little thing really ticks me off. I yell and scream at everyone. My friends are afraid of me. I even scare myself."

Circle the feelings you experience most intensely in your grief:

anger	helplessness
sadness	frustration
depression	shock
hopelessness	numbness
guilt	confusion
loneliness	fear
jealousy	relief
exhaustion	

As you circle a particular feeling, jot down ways you might help yourself cope with that feeling.

Join the other members of your group and create a collage. Each person picks one or two feelings and draws a presentation of each of those feelings on a large sheet of paper. Write in large letters "Feelings of Grief." (Your leader may show you a sample from Appendix C.)

As you look at the collage, talk about additional ways you can cope with some of the other feelings of grief.

Be a friend to yourself by listening to your pain. Honor it. When possible, share it with someone who will be understanding and supportive. (30 minutes)

Activity Sheet 10.1, page 2   Helps in Moving Through Your Grief, Part 2. Permission is granted to photocopy for grief group use. Source: Adapted from *Children and Grief,* by J. W. Worden. Copyright © 1996 by Guilford Press, New York. Used by permission.

Activity 10.1   HELPS IN MOVING THROUGH YOUR GRIEF, Part 3 (Teen Copy)

Task 3. In dealing with the third task of grief, *to adjust to an environment in which the deceased is missing,* it is helpful to address the many changes in your life.

a.   *External Adjustments*—The person who died may have performed a variety of roles in the family. Some are tasks needing to be done by someone else; others are roles not easily filled.

List some things that person did:

Write the names of the persons who now do some of those tasks:

What roles are not yet filled?

What do you miss the most?

b.   *Internal Adjustments*—The loss of a loved one affects one's sense of self. You will most likely continue to explore the question "Who am I?" as part of the mourning process.

In what ways does your grief affect your self-confidence and appreciation of self?

If you feel helpless, is it possible to remind yourself that this is a normal part of the mourning process and you can grow through it?

c.   *Spiritual Adjustments*—Our assumptions about the world are often shaken when a loved one dies. Comment about how any of these beliefs have been challenged.

The world is a benevolent (safe) place.

The world makes sense.

I am okay.

As you explore these beliefs, talking with a non-judgmental person can be a valuable help.
(40 minutes)

Activity Sheet 10.1, page 3   Helps in Moving Through Your Grief, Part 3. Permission is granted to photocopy for grief group use. Source: Adapted from *Children and Grief,* by J. W. Worden. Copyright © 1996 by Guilford Press, New York. Used by permission.

Activity 10.1 HELPS IN MOVING THROUGH YOUR GRIEF, Part 4 (Teen Copy)

Task 4. In dealing with the fourth task of grief, *to emotionally relocate the deceased and move on with life,* spiritual or cultural services help us remember the richness of a person's life.

a. Often, but not always, these take place shortly after the person has died—sometimes on the anniversary of the death.

- In what ways has your family commemorated your loved one's life?

- What parts of the commemoration really reflected what you thought about the person who died?

- Were there any aspects of the service which seemed strange to you? Explain.

- Since your loved one died, describe any times you may have felt connected with that person, such as through dreams, sensing the person's presence, memories, services, family gatherings, photo gathering, and so on.

b. As you move through the painful feelings, as well as when you begin to address some of the challenging issues, life can begin to take on a new meaning. It is okay to move on, while still carrying the memories of the person who died.

- List the fun times you have had during the past month. What are some events that show that you are participating in life?

- Although you may want to move on, in what ways is it difficult to do so?

(35 minutes)

Activity 10.2 CHOOSING TO WORK WITH YOUR GRIEF

Goal

To help teens recognize that their choice to work through grief affects the outcome.

Objectives

To guide the teens in reflecting on how they cooperate in order to accomplish something.

To instruct teens in how they can cooperate in moving through their grief effectively.

Procedure

1. Make one copy of Appendix D, "Crisis: Danger and Opportunity," and multiple copies of Activity Sheet 10.2, "Choosing to Work With Your Grief."

2. Talk about the following:

   Crisis: danger and opportunity, showing the Chinese characters.

   Grief does not just "go away."

   Accomplishing a goal.

   The "work of grief" or "griefwork." Have teens fill in sheet and discuss.

   (20 minutes)

Activity 10.2   THE WORK OF GRIEF (Teen Copy)

Grief does not just "go away." If a person wishes to experience the fullness of living again, it is necessary to engage in the "work of grief." There are two Chinese characters for the word *crisis:* danger and opportunity. Grief is referred to as a "dangerous opportunity." There is a *choice* involved in order to move through grief in a healthy way that leads to growth.

Investing in a Goal

1. Think of something you or someone else would like to accomplish (e.g., swim at the Olympics, play soccer on a traveling team, play the piano or the drums, learn Spanish for your vacation in Mexico). Write what you would like to accomplish.

2. List what it would take to accomplish this goal.

   • How much time would be needed for practice?

   • Who would be involved?

   • What are the expenses?

3. Share what you have written with the group.

Investing in the Work of Grief

Explain that *grief work* requires:

• *Time* to think about the person who has died and what is happening in your life.

• *Commitment* to learn about the grieving process and how it affects your life.

• *Willingness* to explore the pain of intense emotions and experience the relief of working them through.

You are not alone. You may already have the support of these persons:

• Leaders of the grief group.

• Other persons in the group who also are grieving.

You may also have:

• Friends or family members who are able to listen, without judging.

• Other professionals—doctors, guidance counselors, clergy/rabbis.

Activity Sheet 10.2   Choosing to Work With Your Grief. Permission is granted to photocopy for grief group use.

Activity 10.3   FISHBOWL: VISUALIZING GRIEF

Goal

To create a positive visual experience of the feelings of grief, understandable to people of all ages.

Objectives

To represent the various feelings of grief by adding drops of food coloring into a bowl of clear water.

To elicit from the participants their connections between the colors and the feelings of grief.

To also elicit the various ways of coping with the feelings, while pouring a small amount of bleach into the bowl each time another strategy is named.

Introductory Comments

This activity, paraphrased from an article in *Forum*, the newsletter from the Association of Death Education and Counseling, could be used in groups of teens, children, or families gathered for a memorial service to culminate a series of sessions, or during any follow-up camp or gathering for families.

Death and grieving can bring enormous changes to individual and family life. This activity demonstrates that "although we experience many feelings and have resources available to help us, we are forever changed."

1. Display a clear glass bowl or fishbowl half filled with water, representing the family members before their loved one died.

2. Invite the participants to share feelings of grief. As a feeling is named, ask what color would best illustrate the feeling. Drop it into the bowl. Continue exploring a vast number of feelings, noting how each addition of color changes the water's appearance.

3. Note the cloudiness of the water after many colors have been added and blended, showing how difficult it is to identify single feelings amid deep grief.

4. Explore what helps people cope with the feelings of grief. Responses might include "talking, drawing, crying, friends, family members. . . ." Pour a small amount of bleach into the bowl as each suggestion is given.

5. Summarize the demonstration of the process of mourning as depicted visually through color. Grief is manifested through many intense feelings. However, there are often resources we can draw upon to help us move through our grief (Allen, Perschy, & Richardson, 2002). (20 minutes)

Activity 10.4 SAND JACKET: EXPERIENCING GRIEF

Goal

To make the experience of grief more understandable for people of all ages.

Objectives

To represent the various feelings of grief by using colored bags of sand.

To elicit from the participants the connections between the sand packets and the heaviness of grief.

To also elicit the various ways of coping with the feelings connected with taking away the packets of sand.

Introductory Comments

1. This adaptation of the Mad Jacket™, which is used by teachers to address issues of anger, has been revised to depict metaphorically the intense feelings people experience when someone close to them dies. "Making grief visible and less threatening helps people see the need to grieve and heal creatively" (Allen, Perschy & Richardson, 2002).

2. Prepare a simple light vest jacket with large pockets, by attaching clear plastic saddlebags to the shoulders, hanging over the front and the back. Also, fill clear plastic bags each with a different color of sand.

3. Invite a participant to wear the vest jacket. Ask the members of the group to name a feeling of grief and choose a color of a sand packet. Slip the packet into one of the large pockets or into one of the plastic saddlebags. Continue eliciting names of feelings, until all 12 saddlebags and pockets are filled. "The participants are able to feel the weight of emotions, see their many colors, and feel the limitation of movement while carrying heavy grief" (Allen et al., 2002).

4. Invite participants to brainstorm healthy ways of exploring grief and lightening one's load. This could include activities or support people.

5. Each person is invited to create a glass container of sand art by layering the various colors, as a reminder of the analogy of one's effort to lighten one's grief. (20 minutes)

Chapter 11

MOVING THROUGH THE PAIN

> Grief can make you feel crazy. Every emotion is let loose and comes flooding in, eroding any sense of balance. The normal routine of the most stable individual can be disrupted by bursting into tears or being totally distracted by the pain of loss. There is no shortcut to make the turmoil disappear. (Perschy, 1989, p. 1)

The challenge of the grieving teen is that of being engulfed in the turmoil of intense feelings at a time when it is so important to look good and be liked by those around you, especially by your peers. Is there any guidance that might help teens with this dilemma?

Experts in the field of grief remind us that it is not enough to go "around" grief; the operative word is "through." An important part of the grieving process is to feel the pain, not in a masochistic way, but in order to learn from it, and allow a resolution to take place.

The grief group is a natural place to explore the many dimensions of feelings. There are various approaches to choose from within this chapter. Some may work better than others for a particular teen. It may be helpful to provide a mixture of approaches.

Leaders are encouraged to be vigilant during the initial meetings so they may identify the emotions causing the most pain. If it is not so apparent, the group could brainstorm feelings, and each person could name those affecting them the most. When words are not enough to touch into the pain of grief, the arts offer vehicles that allow emotions to surface and promote their expression. Facilitators are encouraged to use various methods, including writing, listening to music, painting, and manipulating clay, in order to assist teens with different learning styles.

11.1 *Journaling* is an effective way of recognizing, naming, expressing, and moving through feelings. Depending on what feelings surface as the teens tell their stories, the facilitators may choose some open-ended sentences, or statements from the journal page, or they may make up their own to put on a sheet. This journal page can help the teens further explore their feelings.

11.2 *How My Life Has Changed* provides the teens with an opportunity to reflect on the losses they are experiencing and how these losses trigger the myriad feelings of grief. Facilitators could follow up with another activity from this chapter that further explores the feelings.

11.3. *Focusing: Listening and Making Friends With Our Feelings* is introduced with a child's story that illustrates the relationship between feelings and how we carry them in our bodies. Facilitators may say something like, "We are becoming more and more aware that our bodies carry our life experiences. This is a way of honoring how we carry our feelings in our bodies and how we can access that wisdom."

Anger and guilt are often the feelings that cause the most pain to those who are grieving.

11.4. *Externalizing Angry Feelings* and 11.5. *Dealing With Guilt* offer practical information and suggested activities to deal effectively with these feelings.

11.6. *Expressing Grief Through Visual Arts* offers unique ways of moving through grief in a more tactile, less verbal way.

11.7. *Expressing Grief Through Music* provides an opportunity for teens to listen to and observe what feelings emerged when certain pieces of music are played. The teens can then use music to work through their feelings at some times, and at other times, they may use music to change how they feel—for example, "What songs can I play to energize me when I am feeling down?"

Activity 11.1 JOURNALING

Procedure

1. Type a few unfinished sentences on a sheet of paper. Make copies, and distribute to the teens.

2. Allow time for the teens to reflect and write their response. Provide time for those who wish to talk about their writing. If no one chooses to share, encourage them to talk with a trusted adult or friend.

I Wish I Had; I Wish I Hadn't . . . (Guilt)

If only I had . . .

If only I hadn't . . .

It was my fault when . . .

I'm so sorry that . . .

I still cannot forgive her/him for . . .

I can't forgive myself for . . .

I am truly sorry for what we never resolved, especially . . .

If we had one more day together, I would . . .

The Many Feelings of Grieving

I am learning that grief affects me physically, emotionally, socially, and even spiritually. The worst part is . . .

There are so many changes since you died, like . . .

I get so angry when I think of you dying because . . .

When I feel lonely, I just want to . . .

I feel sad when I remember . . .

I get so jealous of my friends when I see them . . .

Sometimes I am negative about myself. If we talked about this, I think you might say . . .

I feel better when I . . .

Activity 11.2   HOW MY LIFE HAS CHANGED

Goal

To help teens explore the difficult aspects of change, resulting from loss.

Objectives

1. To help teens identify some changes they have experienced since their loved one died.

2. To encourage the teens to name the feelings connected with the changes and explore new ways of dealing with them.

Introductory Comments

When someone dies, people speak of a sense of loss. "I miss him. Life isn't the same any more." Besides the sadness, loneliness, and turmoil, there are often practical changes that take place. Who will fulfill the tasks the deceased person used to perform? How has our financial situation changed? Sometimes these changes are subtle, and the survivors are not even aware of the impact these changes are having on the family members.

Procedure

1. Introduce the statement, "The *death* of a loved one results in *loss and change.*"

2. Ask the teens, "How are things different in your life since your loved one has died?" List the following categories on a chalkboard or on a large sheet of paper. As the teens name changes, add them next to the category:

   family
   friends
   activities
   school   (10 minutes)

3. Fold a sheet of paper in half. Draw a picture of your family around the table before your loved one died. On the other half, draw a picture of your family today. Reflect on:

   The similarities in the two pictures are . . .
   The differences in the two pictures are . . .
   What I miss the most is . . .
   The changes that bother me the most are . . .
   Allow time to share with a partner, or with the group.   (20 to 30 minutes)

   These questions may trigger strong feelings. Follow the discussion with another activity from this chapter. Remind the teens to take care of themselves.

Activity 11.3   FOCUSING: LISTENING AND MAKING FRIENDS WITH OUR FEELINGS

Goal

To demonstrate for teens how they can be friends with their feelings.

Objectives

1. To encourage the teens to be compassionate toward themselves, while listening to difficult feelings.

2. To help teens be with difficult feelings in a caring way, allowing the story to unfold and some resolution to occur.

Introductory Comments

People often wish to run from the painful feelings of grief, wanting just to get rid of them as quickly as possible. Yet the pain of grief usually lasts longer than anyone ever anticipates. Many theorists in grief studies say how important it is to experience the pain in order to move toward some resolution or healing.

The process of focusing is a valuable tool in assisting persons struggling with intense feelings. A trained guide leads a person in a non-intrusive manner, encouraging that person (focuser) to notice the body feel of a particular emotion and honor it, allowing the story behind it to unfold. The skilled guide, then, continues to accompany the focuser through this healing process. However, it is also possible to guide oneself by "noticing and nurturing" what is real for us.

This level of listening is demonstrated in the children's book *Sadie Listens: An Inward Journey*, as Sadie tries to move beyond the pain of her cat's death. In the foreword, McMahon and Campbell wrote, "We spend huge amounts of time and effort to distract ourselves from the quiet body-knowing beneath our busy thinking" (Steele, 2002, p. III). For more information, go to the website www.biospiritual.org.

Procedure

1. Read the story *Sadie Listens* to the group. Talk about what happened to Sadie when she paused long enough to listen in a friendly way to how she was carrying the pain in her body. Continue talking about how it is possible to receive the wisdom of our bodies. It may not happen the first time we pause and listen. However, with practice we can learn to honor our feelings and allow a natural resolution to occur.

2. Guide the teens in acknowledging a feeling they may have and noticing how they may be carrying it in their bodies. Suggest that they honor where they are carrying it, and see if they might begin to get a sense of some wisdom and/or relief, like Sadie did.

3. Encourage the teens to continue "noticing and nurturing" the body feel of an emotion during the week. (25 minutes)

Activity 11.4   EXTERNALIZING ANGRY FEELINGS

Goal

To help teens learn more about anger and how to express it.

Objectives

1. To identify triggers of anger.

2. To increase the repertoire of ways of dealing with the angry feelings.

Introductory Comments

Often grieving people express concern about the intensity of their anger. Anyone can be the target: friends, doctors, nurses, hospital staff, family members, God, or even the person who died. Elisabeth Kübler-Ross, a pioneer in working with dying persons and their families, recognized anger as a natural result of experiencing a major loss. She believed that pent-up feelings lead to illness and that the externalization of anger is helpful in working through these feelings. Kübler-Ross encouraged people to pound out their anger and resentment in her workshops.

There are many ways of externalizing anger. Vigorously swimming released the intense anger of a 15-year-old boy after his best friend died of leukemia. Another teen skateboarded by the hour whenever he missed his dad. A tall, slender, agile 16-year-old girl poured her energy into her ballet practices after her brother's suicide.

Although punching another person may provide a powerful emotional release, the consequences may bring even more pain. A healthy outlet does not endanger another or oneself. When the anger is continually destructive, adults need to assist the teen in getting professional help. A grief group may not be enough.

Procedure

1. *What makes me so angry?* Ask the teens if any of these quotes sound familiar to them. Allow them to explore their angry feelings. Identifying the triggers of angry feelings is an important first step.

   Nothing in my family is the same anymore.

   "Lighten up," my friends say. But what do they know? Their dads are still alive and well.

   I'm angry all the time. I even scare myself. The slightest thing ticks me off. I'm always yelling at my family and my friends. No one wants to be near me.

   It's all that stupid doctor's fault. Why didn't he find the tumor earlier, before it was too late?

   Dad drank beer, and ate junk food, day in and day out. He was a real couch potato. He just ignored what everyone said about cholesterol and exercise. His heart just gave out. (10 minutes)

2. *Specific ways to express anger.* Talk about healthy ways of expressing anger. Add some of these:

Write down what angers you on a paper; scrunch it up; and throw it into a basket or tear up an old phone book.

Pound a foam bat at something.

Go to the bowling alley; give the pins a person's name or a situation before you roll the ball.

Take a half-dozen eggs into the woods; choose a tree and wham those eggs against that tree. (The birds will appreciate it.)

Yell. Choose a sound-proof spot, or those around you may panic and begin imposing restrictions. (10 minutes)

3. Depending on the meeting place, involve the teens in some active expressions of anger, such as scrunching the paper, pounding the air, vigorously flying paper airplanes, drawing an angry picture, listening to angry music, molding a piece of clay with angry movement, or forming clay into an angry figure. (15 to 20 minutes)

Activity 11.5 DEALING WITH GUILT

Goal

To help teens learn more about guilt, and how to express it.

Objectives

1. To identify causes of guilt feelings.

2. To explore ways of dealing with guilt feelings.

Introductory Comments

Guilt feelings often accompany grief. Death is final. The survivors cannot complete that last disagreement. The "I love you" goes unsaid. The "I'm sorry" is unspoken. The embraces, the good times, are no longer a part of our lives. Sometimes the ending is abrupt.

Feelings of guilt can continue to plague grieving persons, long after the death of someone close. For many, it is more difficult to identify and talk about their guilt than their anger. Therefore, these suggestions could fall flat with little or no response. However, some teens may be ready to address these issues of guilt.

How can we help teens grapple with guilt as they put their relationship with the person who has died in perspective? These activities are designed to help teens pinpoint the causes of the guilt feelings, determine whether or not they were truly at fault, and explore various ways of moving through the pain.

Procedure

1. *What is there to be guilty about?* Read these two sample scenarios to the teens, or if appropriate, use an example from your own life. Ask the teens if they can recall stories of people feeling guilty after someone died, such as in the movie *Ordinary People*, when the brother felt guilty that he lived and his brother died. Many people have guilt feelings after someone dies.

   Talking about guilt can be embarrassing. Therefore, facilitators need to remind teens of the ground rule of confidentiality. The leader could set the tone by sharing a personal issue, or a comment like: "I've heard of bereaved persons who shared harsh words with their loved one before they died, and wound up regretting it long afterward." This exercise gives teens a chance to recall those moments of regret and learn how to move beyond the guilt.

2. *Am I truly to blame?* Help the teens determine whether or not they were really blameworthy. Have them ask themselves, "Did I truly have control over the situation, or am I assuming guilt for something I could not help?" These scenarios may offer some clarity.

   "I let my friend use my car. If only I had said no. Then he would be here now." (You made the decision to lend your car based on what you knew then. You cannot hold yourself responsible for the drunk driver who ran into your friend.)

"If only I could have done more. Should I have nagged dad to go see a doctor for his headaches? I never even checked on him the night that he died of an aneurysm." (People have headaches for many reasons. You didn't know how serious this one was; nor did anyone else in your family.)

"My dad always yelled at me when I stayed out late. Saturday he called me a no-good tramp. He had been drinking. I screamed back at him. I told him that I hated his guts. That night he had a heart attack. I cannot forgive myself."

"I wasn't there when my mom died. None of us were. Dad and I went home to shower and take a break after being at the hospital for two days straight. Then she died. I just feel terrible that I wasn't there."

As they respond to these scenarios, help them determine what was beyond their control, and what reflects their true actions.

3. *Exploring ways to move beyond the guilt.* As the teens are able to distinguish between guilt feelings because of not being able to control the situation, and a true sense of blame, the following sections can help them deal with the feelings:

When we feel guilty for what we couldn't control. Things happen that are beyond our control. We are human, and therefore limited. It is inappropriate to assume the blame for something that was impossible for you to know or do. We are incapable of predicting the future, running someone else's life, or being with one person indefinitely.

What helps?

• Write affirmations, and repeat them to yourself often: "I did the best that I could under the circumstances." "I cannot predict the future, or I cannot control another person's life."

• Talk with a nonjudgmental friend or counselor to put it in perspective.

When our guilt feelings reflect our true actions. When you recognize that you have said some things, and acted in ways that you wish you hadn't, it is normal to feel guilty. Everyone makes mistakes; no one is perfect. We now have the opportunity to forgive ourselves, by offering ourselves the same compassion that we would give to another.

What helps?

• Write a letter to the person who has died, expressing your regrets. Then write another letter as you picture your loved one responding to you in a compassionate way. Continue the correspondence. Discuss with the group, a friend, or counselor any insights you have received.

• Reflect on and write a response to some of the other journaling ideas in this chapter.

• Some issues may be deep and longstanding, and may require help from a professional counselor, or a guide, trained in a spiritual discipline consistent with your own.

Activity 11.6   EXPRESSING GRIEF THROUGH VISUAL ARTS

Goal

To explore with the teens various ways of expressing grief through the visual arts.

Objectives

1. By participating in painting, molding clay, and drawing, teens can learn to be with difficult feelings and move through them.

2. To increase the self-esteem of grieving teens by encouraging them to use their creative ability.

Introductory Comments

Kathie explained that she is not a very verbal person, so her art was the easiest way for her to express herself. "I get lost in my art and paint for hours and hours," she said.

After her husband died, she recalled, "I knew I was suffering, I needed to paint. I had to see the anger; visualize the anger. It was like admitting, 'Yes, *I am* angry.' However, I didn't want anyone else to see it," she admitted. "Sometimes I would become embarrassed, and I would try to change the painting so it wouldn't look angry. Then it looked like it had makeup on it. It was no longer true." Eventually, twenty paintings later, the paintings were happier. As she looked at a woman floating with arms outstretched, Kathie was surprised to see how different this painting was compared to the original ones.

Although Kathie is an adult, expressing feelings through art can be helpful at any age. Art allows us to connect with what is real within ourselves. As we create what resonates with our inner truth, we can more freely move through the pain of our difficult feelings.

Painting Images of Feelings

Ask the teens to notice how they are feeling. Have them look at the colors of markers or paints and choose a color that matches how they feel. Encourage them to draw a picture, or just allow their brush or marker to move in any free-flowing way. Suggest that they add other colors, if they wish. Have them stay with the feeling, reflecting on what they drew. Allow time to talk about how the picture looks and what it felt like to do this activity. (15 to 20 minutes)

Allowing the Clay to Speak

The soft wet feel of molding a piece of clay can help a person reflect on and connect with how he or she is feeling. These are a few suggestions; more ideas may evolve.

Continue molding, allowing a rhythm to develop.

Pound the clay angrily. Or just stay with the lonely, sad, or content feelings as you move the clay.

Make a symbol that matches how you feel, such as flame to represent the fire of anger, a bowl to portray the feeling of emptiness, or a rock to symbolize numbness. You could be with your object in a caring way, or decide to smash it. Go with how you feel.

Create a symbol of a memory of the person who has died. Allow time to talk about the experience. (25 to 35 minutes)

Activity 11.7   EXPRESSING GRIEF THROUGH MUSIC

Goal

To expose the teens to music as a means of working through their feelings.

Objectives

To support teens as they use music to stay with and explore their real feelings.

To encourage teens to listen to music when they would like to change their moods.

Introductory Comments

When interviewing grieving teens about what helped them deal with their feelings, one young woman said that she listened to music. "I don't feel so alone when I listen to sad music. When I'm angry, I like loud music. It reminds me that there are a lot of frustrated people out there" (Perschy, 1989, p. 3).

Music can have a powerful influence on our emotions and even on our bodies. Research conducted by Dr. Helen Bonny showed that music lowered patients' heart rate and blood pressure, and significantly changed emotions from negative to positive on the Emotional Rating Scale (Merritt, 1996).

People who are grieving can use music both to *connect with the feelings* and to *change them.*

Music Can Help Us Be With Our Difficult Feelings

An important task of grieving is to be with the painful feelings. Grieving people talk about how often the demands of daily living consume their attention. Yet they forge ahead, ignoring the screams of the anger, the loneliness, or the guilt feelings.

Our numbed, emotional life can be unthawed, and we can recapture the zest for living. First, we need to acknowledge and be with whatever feelings we are experiencing. This may be unpleasant initially; however, entering into the struggle can heal the pain.

Music can help by letting the feelings flow.

> When conditions seem too frightening to let out your feelings, they can invite music's gentle nudge to help you express them. As you allow the music to help you experience pain and sadness, all the locked up joy bursts forth too, releasing a vitality that kindles interest and excitement in all aspects of your life, your work, your relationships, your studies. (Merritt, 1996, p. 27)

Music Can Relax, Renew, and Soothe

There are times when we cannot take time out to listen to our feelings and allow their full expression. The assignment needs to be completed. The SATs are scheduled for tomorrow morning. The customers at the clothing store where we work want our undivided attention. Music can help us temporarily change our mood.

Music can stimulate or calm us. "If the tempo gets faster, our hearts will beat faster," according to Stephanie Merritt. "If you want to calm down, you would use music with a slower tempo" (Merritt, 1996, p. 121).

Stephanie Merritt also suggested:

> If you are feeling edgy, irritable, or hyper, start with a piece of music that is not too quiet, so that you are able to resonate with it and perhaps give some of your anxiety over to the music. Later, you can switch to a more tranquil piece of music. (Merritt, 1996, p. 147)

Because each person is unique, the following activity will customize each person's response to a particular piece.

Procedure

1. Duplicate the teen copy, "Expressing Grief Through Music," and distribute it. Demonstrate how music can help us stay with our feelings, and can also change our moods. Use music from a favorite movie or ask teens to bring in CDs or audiotapes of a favorite song. It may be wise to set boundaries in the choices, such as no profanity or explicit sexual language.

2. Ask teens to write the name of the piece on their sheet. Play a selection. Ask the group to write words or draw about how they feel physically and emotionally. Talk about it. Vary the music. Ask them to keep track of how they feel as they listen to each selection.

3. Encourage the teens to continue the process at home for five minutes, and then write down how they feel. Have them arrange their list of emotions into categories that could include, but not be limited to, anger, sadness, calmness, and excitement. At the next meeting, ask the group members to share responses.

4. Discuss the possible uses of such a list to *match our feelings* and allow their expression, and to *change them* to provide a better balance in our daily lives. During the discussion, weave in the fact that this may not be an effective tool for everyone. Also, the change could be very slight. Of course, listening to music cannot be a substitute for seeing a mental health professional when the low feeling is intense and has been present for a long time.

5. Emphasize the note at the bottom of the teen copy.

Note: Since this activity may be used during more than one session, no specific time is indicated.

Activity 11.7 EXPRESSING GRIEF THROUGH MUSIC (Teen Copy)

General Information

Music can affect how we feel.

A. *Stay with feelings.* When you feel the intensity of your grief, take some time to be alone. Choose music that matches your feelings. Stay with it. Be with the feelings in a caring way. You could also draw, paint, write, move around. Then create your own music on an instrument, or on makeshift ones such as pots and pans, spoons, wooden blocks, or any nonbreakable objects around the house.

You could end by listening to calming music to give yourself a better balance. Write about the experience in your journal, or talk to a trusted person.

B. *Balancing your moods.* You can also change your feelings. If you feel low and wish to have more energy, play something with a faster beat. When you wish to relax, choose something slower. Consult the *Music List* you have created when choosing a piece.

Music List

Because each person responds in his or her own unique way, listen to your favorite pieces of music. Before a piece begins, jot down how you feel; then do it again, after you have listened. Continue the list on the back of this piece of paper or in your journal.

NAME OF SELECTION   BEFORE   AFTER

Word of caution. You may have difficulty moving beyond the intensity of the feelings while connecting with some music. There are concerns that such music may increase suicidal tendencies. Limit hard-metal rock and vary your musical selections. A teen hotline and a mental health professional would be helpful in supporting you as you move beyond the pain that draws you to consistently choose this music. Reach out for help.

Activity Sheet 11.7   Expressing Grief Through Music. Permission is granted to photocopy for grief group use. Source: Adapted from *Mind, Music, and Imagery: Unlocking Your Creative Potential,* by S. Merritt. Copyright © 1996 by Aslan Publishing, Santa Rosa, CA. Used with permission.

Chapter 12

CONTINUING BONDS: COMMEMORATING AND CONNECTING WITH THE PERSON WHO DIED

New Perspective in Grief Theory

Some of the earlier beliefs regarding the relationship between a person grieving and the one who died had been based on Freud's famous paper, "Mourning and Melancholia." Freud claimed, "For grief to be resolved, emotional energy must be withdrawn from the deceased and reinvested in something new." He went on to say, "One must sever the tie, end the relationship."

Even though "severing the tie" was considered to be the healthy way to "recover" from the pain of grief, that theory is now being vigorously challenged. Research, particularly studies involving bereaved children and teens, is revealing that "they developed a set of memories, feelings, and actions that kept them connected to their deceased parent. Rather than letting go, they seemed to be continuing the relationship" (Klass, Silverman, & Nickman, 1996, p. xvii). People of all ages show a similar pattern. Hence we have the emergence of "continuing bonds" theory. The subtitle of the book *Continuing Bonds* is *New Beginnings of Grief.* Indeed, this is an important change in grief theory.

Ashley Prend summarized this change in her chapter on "synthesis" in her book *Transcending Loss*. "My position is that you cannot and should not sever the ties. Your loved one is in your heart, in your soul, and wrapped intrinsically into who and what you are. You will spend the rest of your life remembering, internalizing, and renegotiating all that this loss means to you in this lifetime. Just because the person is dead, it doesn't mean that your feelings or the relationship dies" (Prend, 1997, p. 64). This is especially true for children and teens. This is an important dimension of the continual process of accommodation that takes place throughout the grieving process.

Practical Ways Children and Teens Have Stayed Connected

The word *accommodation* is often used to describe the many adjustments people make as they mourn the death of a loved one. In their study of grieving children, Silverman and Nickman defined accommodation as "a continuing set of activities related both to others and to shifting self-perceptions, as the child's mind and body change, that affect the way the child constructs meaning." One aspect of accommodating is the way children and teens continue to connect with the person who has died. This connection changes as the young person develops (Silverman & Nickman, 1996, p. 85).

During the Harvard Child Bereavement Study, researchers observed five ways children were able to connect with their deceased parent:

- Locating the deceased.
- Experiencing the deceased.
- Reaching out to initiate a connection.
- Remembering.
- Keeping something that belonged to the deceased (Silverman & Nickman, 1996, p. 76).

How Can Facilitators Foster the Establishment of a Continuing Bond?

Attig has described grieving as a process of moving from "loving others in their presence" to "loving them in their absence," figuratively creating a "place in the heart" in which ongoing contact with memories of the deceased is possible (Attig, 2000, p. 37).

Many grieving children seek to create a *place in their hearts* for their deceased loved one. Worden and Silverman found that "they did so through dreams, by talking to or frequently thinking about their deceased parents, by believing that their dead parents were watching them, by keeping things that belonged to their dead parents, and by visiting their parents' graves" (Silverman & Worden, 1992, p. 100).

As facilitators of grief groups, we can create a safe place for teens to explore this very personal part of their grief journey. Through a variety of activities, leaders can provide opportunities for teens to explore how they have been constructing an inner representation of their loved one, and ways they might continue to create a place in their hearts for their loved one.

There may appear to be some repetition in the following activities. Yet, assuming that the facilitator will only be using one or two, the same concept may be developed in more than one activity. These are only suggested ways of approaching the subject of "continuing bonds." Feel free to adapt, shorten, add your own, and most importantly take your cues from the teens. An activity is only a catalyst. If one small part elicits an open discussion of this sensitive topic, there may not be a need to complete the whole activity. Stay where the energy is.

12.1 *Journaling: Continuing the Dialogue* includes ideas from four categories: remembering, relationship with the loved one, locating a loved one, and holidays. A journal page of any of these themes could enhance any of the other activities in this chapter.

12.2 *Sharing a Memento* is a way of having the teen introduce the loved one to the group members. It highlights additional ways of remembering the person.

12.3 *Ritual* explores the ways we can honor those whose memory is important to us.

12.4 *Family Remembering Album* offers the opportunity for families to gather in order to create a visual story of their family history including the person who has died. This can be done in a setting with other families as a follow-up to a group at a camp or retreat setting. Once families have begun to create pages using everyone's talents, the enthusiasm is contagious. When they are provided with extra supplies, families are more apt to continue to work together at home.

Activity 12.1   JOURNALING: CONTINUING THE DIALOGUE

Goal

To help teens explore their relationship with the person who died.

Objectives

To enable the teens to reflect on their relationship before the person died.

To encourage the teens to explore their continuing relationship.

Introductory Comments

Many suggested journal-type ideas are included in this section. Choose what fits for a particular group of teens. Add your own, based on your observations of the teens.

Procedure

1. Type one of the following sections, allowing space for the teens to write in between the questions. Make copies for the teens. Encourage the teens to read all the items and respond to the parts that make the most sense to them.

2. Provide time for sharing, reminding the teens that they are welcome to "pass" if they feel the material is too private.

3. Have the teen place the paper in his or her own journaling folder as described in chapter 9.

Section A: Remembering and Sensing

Directions: Picture yourself writing a letter or email to the person who died. Include some of your reflections on the following statements:

I recall a funny thing that happened when we were together.

I remember doing some of my favorite things with you.

Since you died, I miss seeing you and interacting with you, especially when . . .

However, I have a sense that we are still connected. I have felt connected in these ways:

What do you think your loved one would say in a return letter? (Use the back of the sheet.)

Section B: Our Relationship: Memories and Legacies

Directions: Read all these unfinished sentences. Answer the ones that make sense to you.

My favorite memory of us was . . .

I am happy that we had a chance to . . .

I wish we could have . . .

A not-so-favorite memory was when . . .

I will always treasure this about you:

Your words that make sense to me now are . . .

There are some things that I do that remind me of our time together:

Section C: Locating Your Loved One

Directions: Sometimes it is helpful to try to get a sense of where people are after they die. Our sense can change, but writing and talking about it has been helpful to many grieving people. Think about and jot down responses to these questions. Then write a letter addressing some of your responses. Then picture your loved one receiving your letter. What do you think he or she would write to you in response? (Use the back of this sheet.)

Have you ever thought about where your loved one might be right now?

What do you think it is like there?

How do you feel about your loved one being in that place?

How do you feel about the person no longer being physically in your life?

Can you locate any of these feelings in your body?

Section D: Holidays, Past and Future

Directions: Holidays are times when we celebrate memories with picture taking, favorite foods, stories, and even music. They are important times of gathering those we love. Choose a holiday that is coming soon. Write about it as if you were talking to the person who died.

My favorite part of the holiday was . . .

The holiday was not always fun. I didn't like . . .

I know it will be different without you. I hope we will still do some things the same as we did before you died. I wish you could tell me how to celebrate without you.

I will miss you particularly when we . . .

I would like to include you somehow. Maybe we could . . .

I would rather commemorate our relationship in my own private way by . . .

Activity 12.2   SHARING A MEMENTO

Goal

To connect with the person who has died though remembering.

Objectives

To emphasize the importance of remembering the person who has died.

To provide an opportunity for teens to share a linking object or a memory with the group.

To encourage teens to find ways of sharing the story of the loved one with others.

Introductory Comments

An important dimension of moving through the journey of grief is for the deceased person to move from an external, physical presence to an internal presence. "Memories and linking objects serve as the bridge between the world with and world without one parent. They evoke feelings of comfort, consolation, and continuity" (Moss & Moss, 1989, p. 110). This could be true whether the person who died is a parent or someone else close to the bereaved teen.

Procedure

1. During the session before using this activity, ask each teen to bring in some memento of the person who has died. It could be something the person owned or something that reminds the teen of that person.

2. Allow time for each person to show and talk about the item and possibly share why he or she brought that particular item. As they take their turn, encourage them to recall an event, a character trait, or something special about their loved one. If the teen forgets to bring something, ask him or her to recall a memory of the person who died.

3. Recognize that keeping and sharing a memento is one way of continuing the relationship with the deceased person; then have the teens explore other ways the teens have found helpful in continuing the relationship.

Possible Questions

What are ways you might have sensed the person's presence?
Is your sense of your loved one the same as or different from a few months ago?
Are there times when you find yourself talking to the person?
If yes, do you get a sense of how your loved one is responding or would respond?
Do you have a sense of whether or not your loved one is able to see you? Hear you?

Activity 12.3   RITUAL

Goal

To help teens explore how ritual can help them connect with the person who died.

Objectives

To provide teens with the opportunity to share information about how they have ritualized their loved one.

To encourage teens to further explore how they might memorialize the relationship they had with their loved one.

Introductory Comments

Ritual offers people a tangible way of dealing with the changes in their lives. When a person dies, the family members usually choose a way of gathering family and friends, as a way of memorializing the loved one and as a way of providing the needed support for the survivors at that very difficult time. Such gatherings usually include a time to share stories about the person. These stories can be very comforting for those attending.

Procedure

1. Talk about the general term "ritual" and what it might mean to the teens. What are some forms of ritual, such as birthday parties, graduations, scouting awards, and military ceremonies?

2. Ask about what kind of rituals they have attended to honor their loved one. Ask them what part was meaningful. What part didn't really make any sense?

3. Talk about how people try to develop a ritual that is meaningful to the attendees. Use an example of how traditionally many couples get married in a courthouse, a church, or a temple. However, we read about weddings taking place underwater while scuba diving, or on the shores of a favorite beach, to signify the couple's connectedness with something they both value.

4. Ask the teens to stretch their imaginations and consider a ritual that would memorialize who their loved one was to them. Where would it be, what would the music sound like, who would attend, how long would it be? Have the teens write a eulogy that highlights that teen's perception of that person.

5. Facilitators could provide the opportunity for the group members to create a ritual that would allow time for each teen to memorialize their special person. If they are willing, encourage the teens to read their eulogies. If the teens are unsure of what to include, the facilitators could offer suggestions, such as lighting a candle. Ask the teens to spend time thinking of the person who has died. What were the special traits? When I think of that person, I feel. . . . A closing could include a minute of silence in thanksgiving for the life of this person. (30–40 minutes)

Activity 12.4   FAMILY REMEMBERING ALBUM

Goal

To gather families in order to create a visual story of their family's history including the person who died.

Objectives

To encourage family members to gather in a casual setting to create within the context of family a memorial to the person who died.

To support family members in recalling, writing about, and creating a visual representation of some important times they spent together.

To provide the material supplies to enable the family to bring this partially completed project home so they can continue to direct their collective energy into a positive healing experience.

Introductory Comments

Rizzuto observed that the process of constructing inner representations involves the whole individual and that these representations are not static, but grow and change with the individual's development and maturation. She also noted the importance of the role of others in the construction of inner representations of significant people in her subjects' lives. Construction, she suggested, is partly a social activity (Rizzuto, 1979, p. 495).

This activity has received "rave reviews" by the families who gathered to create an album to memorialize their loved one. The social aspect is as important as the final product. The ongoing nature of the project allows the opportunity for family members to look back at what they wrote and drew and created at this particular time.

Preparation

1. Call each family, explain about the album, and ask the parent or guardian to bring 10 to 15 photos of the family, including the person who died, along with a pair of scissors.

2. Purchase an album for each family. A standard 8½″ × 11″ album with plastic (acid-free) sleeves holding a sheet of plain paper works well. Also buy decorative stickers, borders, markers, colored paper (8½″ × 11″), glue sticks, scissors, two-sided tape, and display them.

3. Prepare a packet of directions for each family.

4. Encourage the facilitators who are familiar with any of the family members to be available.

Procedure

1. Paraphrase the explanation of the project from the family packet.

2. Distribute a packet and an album to each family. Point out where the rest of the materials are located. Explain some of the directions from the packet.

3. Move around the room stopping at tables, allowing the family members to talk about what they have created.

4. When the time is coming to an end, encourage families to take home extra supplies to continue the project. (90 minutes)

Activity 12.4   FAMILY REMEMBERING ALBUM PACKET
(Family Copy)

An important aspect of the journey though grief is remembering and commemorating the life of the person who has died. Creating this album as a family may help to gather the energy of grief into a positive healing experience. Recalling memories of your relationship together may tap into the inner pain and allow its expression. It may also touch the joy that may have been an important aspect of your relationship with that person.

1. Have each family member choose one or two pictures. Take the white sheet out of the plastic sleeve. Use that sheet or choose a colored sheet. With two-sided tape attach the picture to the page. Choose stickers or borders from the supply table that fits your memory of the event in the photo; for example, add animal stickers to the picture from the trip to the zoo.

2. Have each person write as much or as little as they wish about the story that this picture depicts. These are a few questions to help spark family memories:

    Who is in the picture?

    Where did it take place?

    When was it?

    What was the occasion?

    What happened before the picture was taken and what happened afterward?

    How did you feel at the time?

    How do you feel about it now?

    Why is this photo important?

    (Sometimes the person who has died had been the "picture taker" in the family. That person may not appear in the photo but was very present to the event.)

3. When you bring the album home, add to it any photos, memorabilia, stories that were an important part of your relationship with this special person. It is okay to include the not-so-favorable memories along with the pleasant ones. If it ever becomes overwhelming, remember your immediate support system, and professional services.

Activity Sheet 12.4   Family Remembering Album. Permission is granted to photocopy for grief group use.

Chapter 13

MOVING ON AND BEYOND: THE SEARCH FOR MEANING

Having talked with a number of colleagues working with grieving children and teens, my sense has been that leaders would like to touch on the meaning-making or belief dimensions of grief and trauma, yet they are cautious. These are a few reasons for their hesitance:

- Not wanting to proselytize or be perceived as proselytizing, and thus violate a teen's religious beliefs.
- Not having time in a six- to eight-week group, when there are so many other dimensions of grief which are more visible and obvious.
- Not knowing what to say or how to begin to talk about this dimension of grief.
- Will the discussion trigger some of their own spiritual conflicts?

However, there are more and more voices reinforcing what many of us believe: that addressing issues of "meaning" can release the tremendous power of the spiritual and religious dimension of the journey. This can lead to healing and a more integrated self.

In "How Could God?" Ken Doka recommends that counselors "allow and witness the struggle. In many cases the [teens'] struggle can be invalidated by others, perhaps family or clergy, who fear the questioning of their own spiritual assumptions" (Doka, 2002).

Yes, for many teens, the *conflicts are there*. The important questions are surfacing. Where is it safe to ask those questions? *How* can teens be encouraged to explore these profound realities that can open the door to a newer and fuller experience of life? *Who* is available to accompany these teens on this aspect of their journey? If facilitators can only touch on the conflicts during the short time they are with the teens in a teen grief group, *who else* could they recommend to accompany teens on their search?

These conflicts and questions may flow from many interrelated perspectives. Some of the more obvious ones are the teen's quest for meaning, the loss of an assumptive world, and faith beliefs, including broader spiritual, as well as more specific religious, ones.

Quest for Meaning

Not only do teens search for meaning in the events of everyday living as part of their developmental stage, but that quest extends beyond adolescence. James Fowler (1981) considered *all humans* to be on a quest for meaning, regardless of religious beliefs. Yet in his introductory comments in *Stages of Faith* he recognized the hesitancy his readers may have to enter into the quest. "Why should I risk potential confusion by opening myself up to look at faith as a human universal?" (Fowler, 1981, p. xii). Yet those who are grieving already know confusion. The status quo has been shaken up. Questions of meaning are an important part of the journey of grief.

Ashley Prend described the final stage of grief work, transcendence, as one of growth. "It is all about finding ways to move on creatively and *to make meaning out of loss*" (Prend, 1997).

Loss of an Assumptive World

Each of us has certain assumptions about the world. Children may "assume it will be kind, protective, safe, consistent, and meaningful. They assume their caretakers will be there to provide love, protection, and meaning" (Goldman, 2002, p. 194). This is true of young children, as well as teens.

These assumptions are often shattered when death impacts their lives. This is particularly evident when a child or teen experiences the complications of a traumatic death, such a "murder, suicide, a fatal accident, or sudden fatal illness, death related to AIDS, suicide and homicide, multiple losses and when a child has been abused, neglected, or abandoned by loved one" (Goldman, 1996, p. 8).

Yet the graphic image of an airplane flying into the World Trade Center in New York City on a bright Tuesday in September of 2001, and the horror that followed, will remain embedded in countless minds. Those present at the disaster were traumatized; families, friends, and coworkers of those who died and were injured were traumatized, and "millions of others in this country and around the world were traumatized vicariously by witnessing the attacks and their aftermath in numerous television replays and extensive media coverage. Despite being more geographically remote and not directly harmed, these viewers also were emotionally wounded" (Gamino, 2003, p. 124).

The *loss of the assumption that we are safe* became so evident in the endless conversations that were permeated with expressions of fear and concern about this tragic event. As one therapist declared, "Every one of my regular clients spent at least half of the next few sessions talking about the impact 9/11 had on them, further complicating their own issues."

Other images, such as those of teens being murdered by their classmates in Columbine, of people being targeted by a local sniper attack, and of bombings and war throughout the world, appear on the television in our living room; these depictions reinforce the message. The evening news plays a part in shattering our assumptions that we live in a benevolent world.

Beliefs, Spiritual and Religious

A study of teens following the death of a sibling determined that "the element of tragedy enters the youth's life, and questions about the absurdity of human existence become personal and for some teens, relentless. [They] often mention that God is the target of their anger" (Balk, 1991, p. 2). These relentless questions about the absurdity of or the meaning of human existence are often intertwined with one's spiritual and religious beliefs. Although spirituality and religion are often used interchangeably, they need to be distinguished from each other.

In *Transcending Loss*, Prend defined *spirituality* as "an awareness of and connection to a sacred power that is greater than the self and yet present in each of us" (Prend, 1997, p. 108). Yet a survey of authorities in spiritual studies and death study specialists showed that the term *spirituality* for many people may not include a belief in God. However, a great majority of these experts did agree that spirituality involves forgiveness, connectedness or community, compassion, hopefulness, and meaning or purpose in life (Mahoney & Graci, 1999, p. 523).

Religion refers to an organized set of beliefs or dogma shared by a defined group. Religion may be part, even a large part, of any given individual's spirituality, but is not identical to it (Morgan, 1988; Doka, 2002). Prend described religion as "the outward, organized manifestation of spirituality" (Prend, 1997, p. 108).

In his study on spiritual change, David Balk wrote: "Bereavement contains all the ingredients needed to trigger spiritual change. It is a dangerous opportunity, producing extreme psychological imbalance, and possessing sufficient intensity and duration to allow for serious reflection." He further stated that "bereavement presents a spiritual challenge that can trigger new efforts to construe meaning" (Balk, 1999, p. 488).

The spiritual and religious conflicts and questions are the seeds for transformation. The "dangerous opportunity" to which Balk referred reflects the Chinese characters for crisis. Yes, wrestling with these important life issues may seem risky, yet they certainly contain the potential for growth. This is a sample of questions teens may be asking:

Spiritual

What is the meaning of life?

What is the purpose of my life?

What is important? What do I really value?

Why did this person die?

Religious

How could God let this happen?

If God is a loving God, then why does God allow suffering and violence anyway?

Is God punishing me?

If God is all powerful, why didn't God cure my mother? How does God decide whom to cure, and whom not to?

If I had only prayed the three days before my dad died, would God have cured him?

As people explore the intangible elements of living, often deeper meaning-of-life issues emerge. "Meaning-of-life" exploration may tap into stories with themes of forgiveness, compassion, community, courage, truth, freedom, guilt, and love.

The activities in this section include ways of assisting teens as they search for what is true for them. The first section provides general guidelines, whereas the rest includes specific activities to help the teens explore their issues.

13.1 *Exploring Beliefs: Guidance and Resources* includes a searing story about a 12-year-old boy whose dad died in a coal-mining accident. He is authentically frustrated with God. Robert Coles didn't respond to the core questions of his frustration and later regretted it. It impressed on him the importance of accompanying someone who is wrestling with his or her deepest beliefs (Coles, 1990). Practical suggestions are made as to how to support those who are reconciling these kinds of conflicts.

13.2 *Journaling: Teens Exploring Their Beliefs* includes specific questions and suggestions to assist the teen in reflecting, writing about, and sharing on this most important topic.

13.3 *Positive Outcomes of Grief* emphasizes the growth dimension of grief. A list of positive outcomes is provided for the teen to check. This activity is better used after the teen has dealt with the initial intensity of grief. Only then can grieving persons relate to the concept that there even are positive outcomes.

13.4 *Choices* encourages the teens to acknowledge the reality of situations, yet recognize that they can choose how they perceive them. Using quotes from Victor Frankl, teens can explore how attitude influences how we grow through life's difficulties.

Activity 13.1   EXPLORING BELIEFS: GUIDANCE AND RESOURCES

In the introduction of *The Spiritual Life of Children*, Robert Coles described a conversation with a boy whose dad was one of twelve who died in a mine cave-in. "Why does He sit back and let that happen—and those operators and owners, they won't apologize, and God must know they won't." Coles acknowledged that he might have let that boy reflect on religion, his sense of it—but other interests, psychological and sociological, held his attention then (Coles, 1990, p. xv).

How much room in a teen grief group is there for any *authentic exploration* of religious beliefs, of spiritual beliefs? Where else *does* this exploration take place? Where else *can* this exploration take place? Faced with a dilemma similar to that of Robert Coles, facilitators may decide to address these issues of meaning, either spontaneously when they come up, or to initiate the *search for meaning* questions to enable teens to reflect on, explore, and discuss what may be most important to them. Even if a leader facilitates only one session of the series of six or eight meetings on the spiritual dimension of grieving, the teens could be reassured that it is all right to acknowledge the issues and be encouraged to find support for this aspect of the journey.

Exploring Beliefs With Teens

How can caregivers provide an inviting atmosphere to explore these life-and-death issues? What kind of support does each person/group need in order to allow themselves to enter into the struggle?

1. *Provide a listening presence.* The very fact that adults are willing to listen attentively without trying to fix or change the teens is valuable. This helps to build a trust level where the teen can gradually move from more superficial issues to the most important and difficult ones.

Providing a "pat answer" to a profound question may actually abort the process. When some adults become uncomfortable with the extensive questioning of teens, there may a tendency to provide a logical explanation to the dilemma. Such a simplistic response may be an attempt to "make the teen feel better" or, in some cases, to try to convince the teen of the "right way" to believe. When family members or faith leaders make statements like "Just accept whatever happens as God's will, and do not question," the teen will quickly learn not to bring up such questions.

The fact that adults will listen may be more important than actual answers. Teens may better be able to live with the questions when they know that it is all right to wrestle with them and that they are not alone during this very challenging time. They may eventually come to realize that there may not be a logical explanation. Often issues around death and trauma defy explanation. These events touch upon the "mystery of the universe." Yet, all the wrestling with the questions is such an important process. Teens then know that they have the capability to explore their beliefs, and can continue to do so until something resonates that is truly authentic for them. In the meantime, they may experience some relief in realizing that they can indeed learn to live with the questions. This realization can be very freeing.

2. *Offering encouragement.* When teens are experiencing the darkest, most painful part of the process, facilitators might offer words of encouragement, such as:

It's natural to question your beliefs during time of crisis.

It's hard to make sense of why something so awful could happen.

It is okay not to know all the answers. However, it is all right to ask the questions.

It is all right to be angry at God. Good friends can be angry at each other at times. God can handle it.

3. *Practical activities.* Refer to chapter 6, "Teens Caring for Themselves."

Explore with teens other life-giving non-cognitive practices.

Guide the group in breathing in universal energy of love.

Begin or end the group with mind, body, spirit exercises, such as yoga.

Activity 13.2   JOURNALING:
TEENS EXPLORING THEIR BELIEFS

Directions

Choose a few questions that fit the issues and themes of the teens in your group. Type each one on a sheet of paper. Distribute to the teens. Encourage the teens to read all of these and begin with the one that resonates the most. Allow time for them to write or even draw about them. Discuss afterward, allowing individual teens to "pass," since the material might be too personal to share. Add completed pages to the journal looseleaf notebook.

Some people find that their spiritual or religious beliefs help sustain them in time of crisis. Are there any such beliefs that are a comfort to you?

Some people find that their spiritual or religious beliefs no longer make sense to them. Do you have any beliefs that no longer resonate with you?

How would you describe your image of your higher power? Has your description changed since your loved one died?

Write a letter to your higher power describing what has been most difficult for you since your loved one died. Write a letter to yourself using your imagination as to how you sense your spiritual being would respond.

Or you may decide to write to the person who has died. Describe what has been most difficult for you since that person died. Write a letter to yourself using your imagination as to how your loved one would respond.

Provide time for teens to share whatever part of their journal writing they are comfortable with sharing.

Activity 13.3   POSITIVE OUTCOMES OF GRIEF

Goal

To acknowledge the difficult parts of grief, yet to recognize that there are indeed positive aspects also.

Objectives

To enable the teens to reflect upon the positive aspects of grief in their own lives.

To become aware that others have experienced positive outcomes as they share their reflections in the group.

Introductory Comments

People expect grief to be painful. Most explanations of the mourning process describe the painful struggles involved. However, research studies of grieving persons, and in this case grieving teens, have shown that many people experience some positive gains as well over a period of time.

It may be important that teens be provided the opportunity to reflect on some of the possible positive outcomes and be encouraged to add any others that are not on the list.

One study, entitled "Positive Outcomes of Adolescents' Experience with Grief," involved 93 teens between the ages of 16 and 22 (Oltjenbruns, 1991). The teens were able to identify areas of growth after having experienced the death of someone "very close" or "somewhat close" within the previous 2 years.

Procedure

1. Describe the study of positive aspects of grief.

2. Make and distribute copies of the exploration sheet, "Positive Outcomes of Grief," and have the teens check all that resonates with them. Encourage them to add any others they have experienced that may not be on the list.

3. Ask the teens to choose three that they can relate with the most.

Activity 13.3   POSITIVE OUTCOMES OF GRIEF (Teen Copy)

We have each heard of someone who has encountered some adversity, yet moved beyond it to do great things:

- We hear about people with no arms who paint beautiful pictures with a paintbrush between their teeth.

- We see Christopher Reeve, a famous actor, still in the limelight, from his powered wheelchair, acting in a movie, sharing his inspirational story after a fall that left him paralyzed.

Many grieving teens have found that there are *positive aspects* to grief. These benefits may be subtle, but they can help us realize that "There is often a silver-lining to difficult events" and "Practically any experience can bring forth growth."

1. Check which of the positive outcomes, if any, you feel were the result of your grief experience?

   _____ Have deeper appreciation of life

   _____ Show greater caring for loved ones

   _____ Strengthened emotional bonds with others

   _____ Developed emotional strength

   _____ Increased empathy for others

   _____ Have better communication skills

   _____ Enhanced problem-solving skills

2. Are there other positive outcomes you could add?

3. Share with the other members of the group. What were the top three, if any, that resonated with you? Would you like to share a further explanation or a story relating to any of your choices?

4. Sit with one of your choices for a few minutes. See if a symbol or picture emerges that fits with that choice. Encourage teens to draw such a symbol or create it in clay.

Activity Sheet 13.3   Positive Outcomes of Grief. Permission is granted to photocopy for grief group use. Source: Positive Outcomes of Adolescents' Experience with Grief, by Kevin Ann Oltjenbruns. Copyright © 1991 *Journal of Adolescent Research, 6*(1), 43–53. Used with permission.

Activity 13.4   CHOICES

Goal

To highlight the fact that there is an element of choice involved in how people move through their grief.

Objectives

To introduce teens to the Chinese symbols for "crisis."

To encourage teens to reflect on some of the inspirational wisdom of Victor Frankl.

Introductory Comments

Most people are familiar with the difficult part of a crisis situation. Yet, there are often hidden possibilities to a crisis, as well, although we may not readily recognize them. The Chinese word *crisis* is written using two characters: one means *danger*; the other means *opportunity*. (See drawing, Appendix C.) Some authors of bereavement studies refer to grief as a "dangerous opportunity."

As people have passed through some of the intense pain of grief, they often discover inner strength, or an appreciation of some aspects of life that they didn't know existed within themselves. Victor Frankl spent many years living the horrors of a concentration camp, watching people endure unspeakable suffering. As he observed and reflected on what people had seen, he developed a theory of transformation described in his best-selling book, *Man's Search for Meaning*. He wrote in the introduction, "I had wanted simply to convey to the reader by way of concrete example that life holds a potential meaning under any circumstances, even the most miserable ones" (Frankl, 1984, p. 12).

Procedure

1. Show the teens a chart of the two Chinese characters for crisis and elaborate upon the power each person has to choose.

2. Display charts, each with a quote from Victor Frankl in different parts of the room. Ask teens to walk over to the chart that they are drawn to. Form a group at each chart to prepare a brief presentation exploring or demonstrating something connected with that quote.

3. Have teens take turns presenting and discussing:

"Man's search for meaning is the primary motivation in his life . . ." (Frankl, 1984, p. 105).

"This meaning is unique and specific in that it must and can be fulfilled by him alone."

"Life ultimately means taking the responsibility to find the right answer to its problems and to fulfill the tasks which it constantly sets for each individual" (Frankl, 1984, p. 85).

"The last of the human freedoms—the ability to choose one's attitude in a given set of circumstances" (Frankl, 1984, p. 9).

"If one cannot change a situation which causes his suffering, he can still choose his attitude" (Frankl, 1984, p. 148).

Appendix A: Signs of Complicated Grief

Persistence of denial with delayed or absent grieving.

Depression with impaired self-esteem, suicidal thoughts, and impulses with self-destructive behavior.

Actual organic disease and medical illness.

Progressive social isolation.

Persistent anger and hostility leading to paranoid reactions, especially against those involved in the medical care of the deceased, or else suppression of any expression of anger and hostility.

Continued disruption of normal patterns of conduct, often with a persistent hyperactivity unaccompanied by a sense of loss or grieving.

Continued preoccupation with memories of the deceased to the point of searching for reunion.

Conversion of symptoms similar to the symptoms of the deceased.

Appendix A: Signs of Complicated Grief. Permission is granted to photocopy for grief group use. Source: From *Understanding Human Behavior in Health and Illness* (3rd ed.), by R. C. Simons (p. 505). Copyright © 1985 by Lippincott Williams & Wilkins, Baltimore. Used with permission.

Appendix B: Be Aware of the Warning Signs (of Suicide)

A suicidal person may:

Talk about committing suicide

Withdraw from friends and/or social activities

Be preoccupied with death and dying

Have a recent severe loss

Experience drastic changes in behavior

Lose interest in hobbies, work, school, etc.

Prepare for death by making out a will and final arrangements

Give away prized possessions

Have attempted suicide before

Take unnecessary risks

Lose interest in his or her personal appearance

Increase his or her use of alcohol or drugs

Appendix B: Be Aware of the Warning Signs (of Suicide). Permission is granted to photocopy for grief group use. Source: American Association of Suicidology. Used with permission.

Appendix C: Feelings of Grief

Appendix D: Crisis: Danger and Opportunity

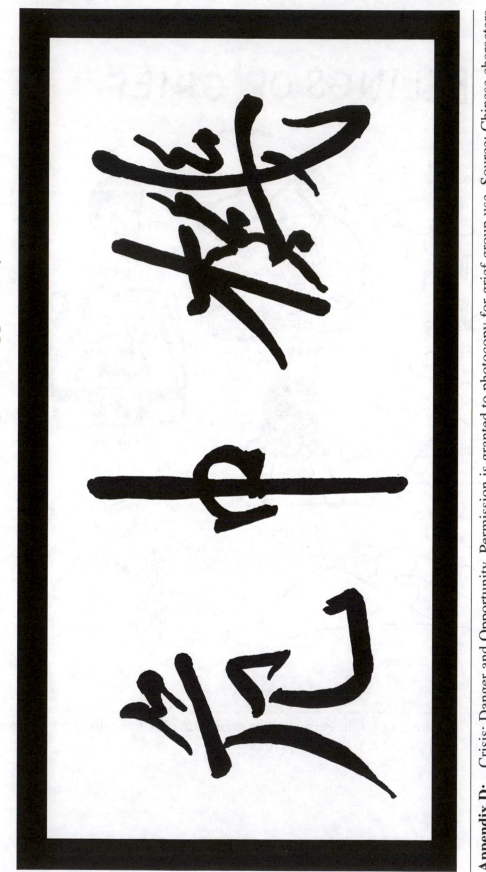

Appendix D: Crisis: Danger and Opportunity. Permission is granted to photocopy for grief group use. Source: Chinese characters drawn by Kathleen Kelly. Used with permission.

Appendix E: Crazy Grief (Teen Copy)

Grief can make you feel crazy. Every emotion is let loose and comes flooding in, eroding any sense of balance. The normal routine of the most stable individual can be disrupted by bursting into tears or being totally distracted by the pain of loss. There is no shortcut to make the turmoil disappear. Wrestling with that grief is the goal of the Teen Support Group sponsored by Hospice Services of Howard County [Columbia, Maryland]. Last October, eight teens ranging in ages from 12 through 16, decided to give this group a try.

The nervousness of the first few sessions melded into a sense of comfort; our group had become a safe place for these teens to move through the grieving process. As my fellow co-leader, Anne Barker, and I approached our sixth meeting, supposedly our last, one group member, Lanisha, asked, "Do we have to stop? I wish this group could go on and on and on." Group members agreed, saying that the group is very important to them in their struggle with loss and they didn't want to lose it, too. Thus, the decision was made to continue the group, meeting twice a month. We agreed to open the group to new members, teens who have experienced the death of someone close to them.

During our first few weeks, we had talked about stages of grief, stress management techniques, and coping strategies during the holidays. We shared our stories about the death of our loved ones and its effect on us. The focus of our eighth meeting was, "What advice would we give a grieving teen?" The teens decided to release themselves from the ground rule of confidentiality in order to include their ideas in this article, wanting their first names used.

The ideas came fast and furiously. "Join a teen grief group to help deal with your feelings," Karyn said. Laurie added with a smile, "Yeah . . . I thought my feelings were dumb and was ashamed of them. Then I came to this group and realized that others have the same feelings. When I am with others outside this group, I feel abnormal. Here I feel more secure. I am a normal grieving person."

Karyn continued, "If there is no group around, choose a friend who you think will stick with you. If you don't have one, find a counselor or psychologist to talk with." This suggestion brought a difference of opinion, with one girl saying, "My friends would probably think I was weird for talking about family problems," and another girl, agreeing with the first, saying, "When I get upset, my friends are there. They let me talk and understand my pain. They also help me get my mind off it all."

Emphasizing the need to deal with one's grief, Fame warned, "Don't block it [grief] out of your mind, or it gets worse. I write about how I feel in my journal. I can do it anytime I want, and it helps." Lisa agreed, adding, "When I get worked up over things, I write about it. I go back and read it later and see how differently I feel. It's encouraging to see how far I've come."

After the initial shock of her dad's death wore off, Laurie decided to try out for roles in a musical at school. She's also writing a story about a child with leukemia which she plans to enter into a short story contest. Fame, too, is focusing her energy on writing; her story features a widow.

Lisa listens to music. "I don't feel alone when I listen to sad music. When I'm angry, I like loud music. It reminds me that there are a lot of frustrated people out there."

Skateboarding helps Jeremy work through his aggression. "When I'm angry or sad, it makes me happy." Jason's involvement in lacrosse, soccer, and running gets his mind off his problems. "I was thinking of giving up ballet after my brother died," shared Mandy. "I couldn't hold back the feelings when I danced. I just cried and cried. But now, two months later, I feel good when I dance. Since ballet demands one-track thinking, I can redirect my energy this way. I'm doing something for me."

The variety of responses highlighted the fact that there is no one way to grieve. Each person develops his or her unique style.

The taboo against crying in public was discussed. Even though tears play a normal part in the healing of grief, they can be extremely embarrassing. "I feel so awkward if something reminds me of my dad and I start crying in school," said Laurie. "I head for the bathroom until I stop, at least temporarily." She added, emphatically, "I'd rather cry alone." Everyone readily agreed.

As the topic changed to ways others could be helpful to grieving teens, the energy level in the room intensified as each person waited to describe the incidents that have been frustrating for them. Underlining the sense of separation that grieving teens experience, much resentment was expressed over comments like, "Aren't you over that yet? Didn't your dad die over a month ago?" "Some people treat me like I have a disease," said Karyn. "They either totally ignore me or, if they do talk, they are afraid to mention the word 'death,' or the person's name." Others in the group complained about people they hardly knew, seeking information, then passing it on to others without a sense of concern.

"If someone would just say they heard my dad died, and did I want to talk, I would know they cared, yet wouldn't feel pressured to respond," says Karyn. "What really helps is a hug from a friend."

One teen, annoyed that her teacher talked about her dad being sick on a day she was absent, said, "It would have been better if the teacher had checked with me first. It was eerie to return to class knowing this information had been shared with kids I hardly knew."

Another teen was offended by her teacher's comment a short while after her dad died. "It's been a month now. You ought to start working on your grades." She explained that it isn't over for her yet. "It is so difficult for me to concentrate. I just wish they could understand."

A favorite analogy of the group is the comparison of grief with a broken leg. People don't expect a person with a broken leg to run a marathon in a month, yet they often expect a grieving person to carry on as if nothing has happened.

Some relatives expect too much. "Now you are the man of the family," said to 14-year-old Jason, infuriated the members of the group. When an adult said, "Take care of your mother," to another girl, she wanted to shout, "What about me?" She explained to the group, "I was afraid they would be shocked by such a selfish statement so I said nothing, but I was seething inside." After describing the incident, she ground her soda bottle into her crackers and slowly articulated, "Don't take my grief away."

It takes courage to grieve in a society that mistakenly values restraint, where we risk the rejection of others by being open and different. Open mourners are a select group, willing to journey into pain and sorrow and anger in order to heal and recover (Tatelbaum, 1980, p. 9).

I have great respect for the courage of these teens who initially took a risk to join a grief group and are continuing to struggle to maintain some balance amid the chaos of grief. Their desire to be there for other teens has greatly inspired me.

Appendix E: Crazy Grief. Permission is granted to photocopy for grief group use. Source: *To Make the Road Less Lonely*, by Mary K. Perschy (1989, Winter). Crazy Grief, pp. 1 & 3. Used with permission.

Appendix F: My Mind, Emotions, and Soul Matured . . . Too Fast for My Years (Teen Copy)

My mother passed away on Memorial Day. That was fitting, really. She didn't serve her country in what people think of as the traditional way, but she did raise three children while fighting an unhealthy and weak immune system. Paulette Frank was one month shy of her 48th birthday.

She was diagnosed with Crohn's Disease soon after her sister Barbara died from complications of the same disease in 1978. She met my father, David Frank, on Jan. 29, 1980. They were engaged in March and married on June 22 that year. He knew her health condition.

The 1980s were a good decade because my mother was relatively well. I was born in February 1983, and she spent all her time with me until I started preschool at 2½. My sister, Alexandra, was born in 1986, and my brother, Louis, in 1988.

In the early 1990s, things started to go downhill. She had her large intestine removed in June 1993. She began to lose weight. Skin usually becomes flabby with weight loss, but hers became tighter.

In late 1993, we found out why: She was diagnosed with scleroderma, a potentially fatal autoimmune disease that causes thickening and hardening of the skin as well as damage to internal organs. There is no cure.

Over time the tightness of her skin relaxed, but the internal damage had taken its toll. She dehydrated at the drop of a hat and was in and out of the hospital.

Upon the family's return from Disney World in July 1999, she was diagnosed with secondary pulmonary hypertension. This constricted the blood vessels in her lungs, making it difficult to breathe and causing her heart to pump three times as fast as it should have.

From then on, she was dependent on oxygen, and that changed our lives. She was no longer allowed to drive. Her friends stopped inviting her to go out. It fell upon me to take her shopping and on excursions.

The week before she died, she was not feeling well. On Thursday she was admitted to the hospital for the usual dehydration. My father and sister returned her to the hospital around midnight on Sunday. By 3:30 that afternoon, she was gone.

The four of us were at her bedside in the intensive care unit as she slipped away. Our reactions were different. My brother and sister stepped back, not saying anything. My father climbed on the bed with her and didn't want to let go. I stepped closer, but didn't touch her, afraid I would hurt her. I was the only one who spoke, but all I could say was, "I love you."

Years of caring for an ill mother shaped me in ways my peers and other people do not understand. As the eldest, I had to take on more responsibility and as a result, my mind, emotions and soul matured at a rapid pace too fast for my years.

My mother's life and death shaped me in such a way that I know who I am. Part of that is knowing that I have a void that will never be filled. Everything I do, every movie I see, every book I read, every concert I go to, I want to tell her about, but I cannot. However, I have a feeling she knows what I want to say and is looking out for me as she always did.

At her graveside, I said these words:

"My mother is a hero to anyone whose life she touched. She seemed to effortlessly care for everyone while masking the pain she suffered. She never complained. She never said a bad word about anyone. She never took anything for granted.

"She taught me more than any textbook or college course. The hardest lesson to understand entails that fairness in life does not exist nor do all people have equal burdens to bear. Most important, I have learned that nothing can destroy the human spirit and the will to live, unless a person allows it.

"My mother refused to give up because she had her children to live for. She continued to suffer the pain of this world for me. Observing such courage and strength, I had no choice but to absorb some of it. She added these qualities to my character and a part of her lives on through me. I will live the rest of my life in her memory and honor. Everywhere I go and everything I do will be because of her.

"Her body may have lost the battle with disease, but I'd like to think her spirit won the war. It's okay, Mom, you won, and I'm glad you're finally at peace."

Appendix F: My Mind, Emotions and Soul Matured . . . Too Fast for My Years. Permission is granted to photocopy for grief group use. Source: *The Washington Post*, by Stephanie Frank. Copyright © 2000 by Stephanie Frank, September 26, 2000. Used with permission.

Appendix G: Amy and Mr. Matthews (Teen Copy)

(The following story is fictional. Names used pertain to no particular person or place.)

Amy Preston just finished sixth grade at Oakdale Middle School. She was a good student and enjoyed school. It was easy to be a good student and like school when you had Mr. Matthews for your teacher. He was not only a good teacher, but a good friend both to students and teachers. Amy would miss having him as her teacher next year.

Every summer Mr. Matthews worked as a camp counselor, up in the mountains, at a camp for physically handicapped children. Each year he gave his students his camp address and encouraged them to write and tell him about their summer vacation. He always answered every student's letter.

Amy suddenly felt an urge to write Mr. Matthews:

July 20, 1999
Dear Mr. Matthews,
    How do you like camp this year? Those kids really are lucky to have you as their camp counselor! Guess what? I'm looking forward to school starting again! I don't know if you heard, but my dad died last month. It was June 26. We were all playing volleyball at a church cook-out and he had a heart attack. Two of our church members did CPR, but couldn't bring him back. The EMT guys got there real fast, but I think he was already gone. It's been real hard for Mom and me, but I know my dad is in heaven. I wish you were here so we could visit and talk. I really enjoyed being in your class last year. I'm looking forward to seeing you soon!
    Love, Amy Jean Preston

July 23, 1999
Dear Amy,
    I was so saddened to hear about your father. I had not heard of his death until I got your letter. Thanks for writing to tell me. As soon as I get back (around the week-end of August 13), I'll call your mother and arrange to come visit.
    Amy, I can't say I know exactly how you feel, but I can tell you that when my wife died (four years ago) I didn't even want to live! It just seemed that life was nothing without her. But I knew she would want me to keep on doing what I was doing. She believed that my work at the school and here at camp were important. Somehow, I was able to go on with my life. I'm glad that I did, because I met you!
    I remember well what a wonderful, loving man your father was. I had much respect for him. I know he felt blessed to have you as his daughter. I also know you will continue to accomplish much in your lifetime. Your life will continue

to bring honor to your father's name. You will be—in fact,
already are—a beautiful, living memorial to your father.

I thoroughly enjoyed having you as a student, and look
forward, as well, to seeing you very soon! God bless you
and your mother.

All the best,
Fred Matthew

Activity to Do at Home or in a Grief Support Group

Pretend Mr. Matthews has come home from camp, called Amy's house, and set a time
with Mrs. Preston for a visit. Write, or act out in a skit, how that visit went. For example,
what feelings do Amy and her mother express to Mr. Matthews? What information does
he share with them about things that helped him the most after his wife died? What does
he say or do that makes Amy feel better? How does the visit end? Do they plan to meet
again, and if so, for what purpose? How do they say goodbye? (Alternatively, the preced-
ing might be expressed by a series of cartoon frames.)

Note to parent or grief facilitator: Fantasizing this scenario prompts participants to
apply creative, problem-solving energy that helps identify what they need themselves for
bereavement support. Further, by relating to the roles in the fantasy, participants experience vicariously hope and encouragement that can carry over to their personal situation.

Appendix G: Amy and Mr. Matthews. Permission is granted to photocopy for grief
group use. Source: From *Bereavement Magazine*, by Yvonne Williams, July/August 1999.
Used with permission.

Appendix H: "Goodbye" Means Ouch! (Teen Copy)

Saying goodbye is always stressful.

If you've ever had to say it, then you've experienced some amount of grief. Certainly the death of someone close causes grief, but so do lesser losses of daily living—only to a smaller degree.

Big losses, little losses; big griefs, little griefs—when you lose something in which you've invested yourself, it always causes stress. It hurts and leaves a wound that must be healed.

Grief is the process of healing that follows the loss. It is natural. And it is necessary.

People react differently to loss, but regardless of how it is expressed, accepting and acknowledging the pain is an important first step in healing. Tolerance within the family for the many forms of expression is important.

If the healing process is short-circuited by refusing to acknowledge suffering, the distress is compounded. When feelings are hidden to numb the pain, the healing process is delayed.

Unrecognized, unhealed grief leaves festering wounds. Unresolved grief is a factor behind a surprising amount of stress-related disease. At least one-third, possibly up to one-half, of people hospitalized are suffering from a recent loss experience. Unfinished grief is a powerful source of distress.

So, what do you do about stress?

Go ahead and grieve.

Grief isn't the problem; it's the solution.

Give yourself permission to grieve.

People who go through surgery usually accept the fact that they won't regain full physical strength for quite some time. Often, however, persons with an emotional loss won't give themselves time to heal. They compound the problem by becoming impatient. You need to give yourself permission to feel the pain that follows loss.

Invest yourself again.

After you've been hurt, it's natural to hesitate making new investments. Grief, however, calls for new investments. Look for people and challenges in which you can reinvest your love and attention.

Use strengths resulting from grief.

Although grief is seldom an experience people choose, it is an opportunity for growth. As a result of your pain, you will find you possess a new set of strengths. Use them to help yourself and others.

Work on your faith.

Loss signals life's impermanence. Grief reminds people of death. Faith helps you deal with others' deaths as well as your own. Every grief experience invites you to renew your acquaintance with the mysteries of life.

Lean on others.

Share you grief with others. It keeps the healing process flowing. Join a group whose members are working through their own grief process and who are committed to caring. Sometimes you can't do it alone. Reach out.

Appendix I: Affirmations

It takes a lot of courage to feel the pain of grief and move through it. I will grieve with purpose.

I know that to face my grief is a way to heal the pain.

I need to let other people support me in my grief.

I will grieve for my special person on and off as I grow up.

I am not alone.

I will survive.

I may not trust everyone, but I can trust some people.

I can find healthy ways to express my feelings.

I can adjust to the many changes of loss, a little at a time.

I have the power deep within me to get through this.

This is the beginning of a transformation.

There will be rocky times and good times.

I can learn from my mistakes.

I can choose to take care of myself.

It is all right to take breaks from my grief, and do fun things.

I can live in the precious present.

I can begin to see the silver lining behind the clouds.

Anger is energy and can be directed in a positive way.

There is a time for everything.

Appendix I: Affirmations. Permission is granted to photocopy for grief group use.

Appendix J: What I Learned About Grief: Teens Speak Out

Don't try to analyze the loss, however long it takes, process it with others, and then let it go. Keeping a hold of the anger will only make you bitter and create future problems. Vanessa, 18

The only way to get over it is to deal with it. Jenny, 15

My respect for others and myself helped me get through bad times. Neil, 16

I just told myself that I could do it. Trista, 15

Just the simple fact that I believe in God and eternal life lets me believe that those who have gone before me are safe, happy, or at peace. Jessica, 17

My loss helped me get in touch with my feelings. Steven, 19

I learned people really cared about me. John, 17

Life is short, live for today. Steven, 19

Appendix J: What I Learned About Grief: Teens Speak Out. Permission is granted to photocopy for grief group use. Source: *Help for the Hard Times: Getting Through Loss* by Earl Hipp. Copyright © 1995, published by Hazelden, Center City, MN (pp. 113–115).

Appendix K: Seven Things a Grieving Person Needs to Know

1. You are lovable even when you are a confused mess.

2. Crying is a gift.

3. Almost every thought, behavior, and feeling is normal.

4. You are not alone.

5. People are uncomfortable with grieving people.

6. No matter how bad you feel, you will survive.

7. It takes as long as it takes.

Appendix K: Seven Things a Grieving Person Needs to Know. Permission is granted to photocopy for grief group use. Source: *Help for the Hard Times: Getting Through Loss*, by Earl Hipp. Copyright © Hazelden, Center City, MN (pp. 63–67).

PART D
RESOURCE MATERIAL

BOOKS

Children's Books That Could Be Used With Young and Old

Buscalgia, Leo. (1982). *The fall of Freddie the leaf.* Bellmawr, NJ: Holt, Rinehart, & Winston.

Johnson, Spencer. (1984). *The precious present.* New York: Doubleday.

Sanford, Doris. (1985). *It must hurt a lot.* Portland, OR: Multnomah Press.

Schwiebert, Pat, & Delyen, Chuck. (1999). *Tear soup: a recipe for healing after loss.* Portland, OR: Grief Watch.

Smith, Doris Buchanan. (1973). *A taste of blackberries.* New York: Harper & Row Junior Books.

Steele, James M. (2002). *Sadie listens.* Glenwood Springs, CO: Steele Studios Publishing Division.

Varley, Susan. (1984). *Badger's parting gifts.* New York: Lothrop.

Viorst, Judith. (1971). *The 10th good thing about Barney.* New York: Atheneum.

Adults Helping Teens

Abrams, Rebecca. (1999). *When parents die: Learning to live with the loss of a parent.* London: Routledge.

Alexander, Debra. (1999). *Children changed by trauma: A healing guide.* Oakland, CA: New Harbinger Publications.

Bernstein, Joanne, & Reedman, Masha Kabahow. (1989). *Books to help children cope with separation and loss: An annotated bibliography.* New York: R. R. Bowker.

Burrell, Rachel, Coe, Barbara, Hamm, Ginger, & Canarie, Beth Cullen. (1994). *Coping with grief at school.* Cincinnati, OH: A Center for Grieving Children.

Corr, Charles A., & McNeil, J. N. (1986). *Adolescence and death.* New York: Springer.

Corr, Charles A., Nabe, Clyde M., & Corr, Donna M. (2000). *Death and dying, life and living* (3rd ed.) Belmont, CA: Wadesworth/Thomson Learning.

Doka, Kenneth J. (Ed.). (2000). *Living with grief: Children, adolescents, and loss.* Philadelphia, PA: Taylor & Francis.

Dougy Center. (1999). *What about the kids? Understanding their needs in funeral planning and services.* Portland, OR: The Dougy Center (www.GrievingChild.org).

Dougy Center. (1999). *Helping teens cope with death.* Portland, OR: The Dougy Center. (www.GrievingChild.org).

Fleming, S. J., & Adolph, R. (1986). Helping bereaved adolescents. In C. Corr & J. McNeil (Eds.), *Adolescence and death* (pp. 97–118). New York: Springer.

Fogarty, James. (2000). *The magical thoughts of grieving children.* Amityville, NY: Baywood.

Fox, Sandra. (1985). *Good grief: Helping groups of children when a friend dies.* Boston: New England Association for Education of Young Children.

Gamino, Louis A. (2003). Critical incident stress management and other crisis counseling approaches. In Marcia Lattanzi-Licht & Kenneth J. Doka (Eds.), *Coping with public tragedy* (pp. 123–138). New York: Hospice Foundation and Brunner Routledge.

Goldman, Linda. (1996). *Breaking the silence: A guide to help children with complicated grief—Suicide, homicide, AIDS, violence, and abuse.* Washington, DC: Accelerated Development.

Goldman, Linda. (2002). The assumptive world of children. In Kaufman, Jeffrey (Ed.) *Loss of the assumptive world: A theory of traumatic loss* (pp. 193–202). New York, NY: Brunner-Routledge.

Grollman, Earl. (1995). *Bereaved children and teens.* Boston: Beacon Press.

Haley, John D. (2002). *How to write comforting letters to the bereaved: A simple guide for a delicate task.* Amityville, NY: Baywood.

Hipp, Earl. (1995). *Help for the hard times: Getting through loss.* Center City, MN: Hazelden.

Jewett, Claudia. (1983). *Helping children cope with separation and loss.* Grand Rapids, MI: Zondervan.

Klass, Dennis, Silverman, Phyllis R., & Nickman, Steven L. (Eds.). (1996). *Continuing bonds: New understandings of grief.* Philadelphia, PA: Taylor & Francis.

Klicker, Ralph L. (2000). *A student dies, a school mourns: Dealing with death and loss in the school community.* New York: Brunner-Routledge.

Malicoat, Trey, & Morris, Amy. (2000). *The journey of change: How to walk alongside a child or adolescent living with death, divorce, or life transition.* Salem, OR: Mother Oak's Child Center for Grieving Children.

Merritt, Stephanie. (1996). *Mind, music, and imagery: Unlocking your creative potential* (2nd ed.). Santa Rosa, CA: Aslan.

Poust, Mary DeTurris. (2002). *Parenting a grieving child: Helping children find faith, hope, and healing after the loss of a loved one.* Chicago: Loyola Press.

Simons, R. C. (1985). *Understanding human behavior in health and illness* (3rd ed.) Baltimore: Lippincott Williams & Wilkins.

Wolf, Anthony E. (1991). *Get out of my life, but first could you drive me and Cheryl to the mall: A parent's guide to the new teenager.* New York: Noonday Press.

Wolfelt, Alan. (2001a). *Healing a teens grieving heart: 100 Practical ideas for families, friends, and caregivers.* Fort Collins, CO: Companion Press.

Wolfelt, Alan. (2001b). *Healing your grieving heart for teens.* Fort Collins, CO: Companion Press.

Worden, J. William. (1996). *Children and grief: When a parent dies.* New York: Guilford Press.

Worden, J. William. (2002). *Grief counseling and grief therapy: A handbook for the mental health practitioner* (3rd ed.). New York: Springer.

Curricula and Manuals

Burrell, Rachel, Coe, Barbara, Hamm, Ginger, & Canarie, Beth Cullen. (1994). *Coping with grief at school.* Cincinnati, OH: Fernside: A Center for Grieving Children.

Cunningham, Linda. (1990). *Teen age grief (TAG).* Panarama City, CA: Teen Age Grief.

Fitzgerald, Helen. (1998). *Grief at school.* Washington, DC: American Hospice Foundation.

Flynn, Nanette, & Erickson, Mel. (2000). *Teen talk: A grief support group for teenagers.* Puyallup, WA: GriefWorks: A Bereavement Resource.

Klicher, Ralph. (1990). *A student dies, a school mourns. Are you prepared?* Buffalo, NY: Thanos Institute.

Lehmann, Linda, Jimerson, Shane R., & Gaasch, Ann. (2001). *Teens together grief support group curriculum: Adolescence edition.* Philadelphia, PA: Taylor & Francis.

Lehmann, Linda, Jimerson, Shane R., & Gaasch, Ann. (2001). *Grief support group curriculum: Facilitator's handbook.* Philadelphia, PA: Taylor & Francis.

O'Toole, Donna. (1989). *Growing through grief.* Burnsville, NC: Mt. Compassion.

Perschy, Mary. (1997). *Helping teens work through grief.* Philadelphia, PA: Taylor & Francis.

Wolfelt, Alan D. (1996). *Healing the bereaved child.* Fort Collins, CO: Companion Press.

Zalaznik, Patricia H. (1996). *Stone soups and support groups: Your guide to a nurturing grief support group.* Minneapolis, MN: Abundant Resources.

Journals for Teens

Caplan, Sandi, & Lang, Gordon. (1995). *Grief's courageous journey: A workbook*. Oakland, CA: Harbinger.

Davidson, Judy. (1997). *Grief skills for life: A personal journal for teens about loss*. Berea, KY: Renew: Center for Personal Recovery.

Dower, Laura. (2001). *I will remember you: What to do when someone you love dies: A guidebook through grief for teens*. New York: Scholastic.

Miller, Jack. (1993). *Healing our losses: A journal for working through your grief*. San Jose, CA: Resource Publications.

Traisman, Enid. (1993). *Fire in my heart, ice in my veins*. Omaha, NE: Centering Corporation.

Wolfelt, Alan D., & Wolfelt, Megan E. (2002). *The healing your grieving heart journal for teens*. Fort Collins, CO: Companion Press.

Books Specifically for Teens Who Are Grieving

Cobain, Beverly. (1998). *When nothing matters anymore: A survival guide for depressed teens*. Minneapolis, MN: Free Spirit Publishing.

Gootman, Marilyne. (1994). *When a friend dies: A book for teens about grieving and healing*. Minneapolis, MN: Free Spirit Publishing.

Graville, Karen, & Haskins, Charles. (1989). *Teenagers face to face with bereavement*. Englewood Cliffs, NJ: Julian Messner.

Grollman, Earl A. (1993). *Straight talk about death for teenagers*. Boston: Beacon Press.

Hipp, Earl. (1995). *Help for the hard times: Getting through loss*. Center City, MN: Hazelden.

Krementz, Jill. (1981). *How it feels when a parent dies*. New York: Knopf.

Le Shan, Eda. (1976). *Learning to say goodbye: When a parent dies*. New York: Macmillan.

O'Toole, Donna. (1995). *Facing change: Falling apart and coming together again in the teenage years*. Burnsville, NC: Companion Press.

Richter, Elizabeth. (1986). *Losing someone you love: When a brother or sister dies*. New York: G. P. Putnam's Sons.

Wolfelt, Alan D. (2001). *Healing your grieving heart for teens: 100 Practical tips*. Fort Collins, CO: Companion Press.

Related Articles, Pamphlets, and Chapters

Allen, Kathy, Perschy, Mary, & Richardson, Mary. (2002, October–December). Gathering grieving families: Three activities. *The Forum*, pp. 6–7.

Balk, D. E. (1981). *Sibling death during adolescence: Self concept and bereavement reactions*. Unpublished doctoral dissertation, University of Illinois at Urbana-Champaign, Champaign.

Balk, D. E. (1983). Adolescents' grief reactions and self-concept perceptions following sibling death: A study of 33 teenagers. *Journal of Youth and Adolescence, 12*(2), 137–161.

Balk, D. E. (1990). The self-concept of bereaved adolescents: Sibling death and its aftermath. *Journal of Adolescent Research*, 6, 7–28.

Balk, D. E. (1999). Bereavement and spiritual change. *Death Studies, 23*(6), 485–493.

Be aware of the warning signs. (2002, March). *Some Facts About Suicide and Depression*. Washington, DC: American Association of Suicidology.

Bishop, G. A. (1990). *Death in a teen's life*. Unpublished manuscript.

Bowlby, John. (1978). Attachment theory and its therapeutic implications. *Adolescent Psychiatry, 6*, 5–33.

Browning, David. (2002). Saying goodbye, saying hello: A grief sojourn. *Journal of Palliative Medicine, 5*(3), 465–469.

Carey, Anne L., Copeland, Delia, & Cryderman, Rick. (1992). The rituals of life that say we belong. *Thanatos, 17,* 13–14.

Cobb, S. (1976). Social support as a moderator of life stress. *Psychosomatic Medicine, 38*(5), 300–314.

Frank, Stephanie. (2000, September 26). My mind, emotions and soul matured . . . too fast for my years. *The Washington Post*, p. C 1.

Garber, B. (1985). Mourning in adolescence: Normal and pathological. *Adolescent Psychiatry, 12*(4), 371–387.

George, Annette. (1984, Winter). Groups make good grief. *Interaction* [newsletter of the Association for Religious and Value Issues in Counseling], *2*, 1–3.

Gray, Ross E. (1988). The role of school counselors with bereaved teenagers: With and without peer support groups. *The School Counselor, 35*(3), 185–193.

Gray, Ross E. (1989). Adolescents' perceptions of social support after the death of a parent. *Journal of Psychosocial Oncology, 7*(3), 127–144.

Hogan, Nancy S., & Greenfield, Daryl B. (1991). Adolescent sibling bereavement symptomatology in a large community sample. *Journal of Adolescent Research, 6*(1), 97–112.

Hogan, Nancy S., & DeSantis, Lydia (1994). Things that help and hinder adolescent sibling bereavement. *Western Journal of Nursing Research, 16*(2), 132–153.

Jacobsen, Gail B. (1990). *Write grief: How to transform loss with writing*. Menomonee Falls, WI: McCormick and Schilling.

Kandt, Victoria. (1994). Adolescent bereavement: Turning a fragile time into acceptance and peace. *The School Counselor, 41*(3), 203–211.

Masterman, Sharon Hale, & Reams, Redmond. (1988). Support groups for bereaved preschool and school-age children. *American Journal of Orthopsychiatry, 58*(4), 562–570.

Moore, Julia. (1992). When your friend's parent dies. *Thanatos, 77*(2), 10–11.

Moss, M. S., & Moss, S. Z. (1989). The death of a parent. In R. A. Kalish (Ed.). *Midlife loss: coping strategies* (pp. 89–114). Newbury Park, CA: Sage.

Oltjenbruns, Kevin Ann. (1991). Positive outcomes of adolescents' experience with grief. *Journal of Adolescent Research, 6*(1), 43–53.

Perschy, Mary K. (1989, Winter). Crazy grief. *To Make the Road Less Lonely,* pp. 1, 3.

Perschy, Mary K., & Barker, Anne. (1990). Teen grief group: Respite from isolation. *Bereavement Magazine, 4*(5), 42–43.

Scravani, Mark. (1992). *When death walks in.* Omaha, NE: Centering Corporation.

Silverman, Phyllis, R., & Worden, J. William. (1992). Children's reactions in the early months after the death of a parent. *American Journal of Orthopsychiatry, 62*(1), 93–104.

Silverman, Phyllis R., Nickman, Steven, & Worden, J. William. (1992, October). Detachment revisited: The child's reconstruction of a dead parent. *American Journal of Orthopsychiatry, 62*(4), 494–503.

Silverman, S. M., & Silverman, P. R. (1979). Parenthood Communications in widowed families. *American Journal of Psychotherapy, 33,* 428–441.

Stevenson, Robert G. (1990). Teen suicide: Sources, signals, and prevention. In John Morgan (Ed.), *The dying and bereaved teenager* (pp. 125–139). New York: Charles Press.

Tekulve, Louise. (1992). The seasons of grief. *Bereavement Magazine, 6,* 12.

Tubesing, Nancy, & Tubesing, Donald. (1983). "Goodbye" means ouch! In *The stress examiner.* Duluth, MN: Whole Person Associates, in cooperation with Aid Association for Lutherans.

Vachon, M., & Stylianos, K. (1988). The role of social support in bereavement. *Journal of Social Issues, 44,* 175–190.

Vachon, M. L. S., Lyall, W. A. L., Rogers, J., Freedman-Leftofsky, K., & Freedman, S. J. J. (1980). A controlled study of self-help intervention for widows. *American Journal of Psychiatry, 137,* 1380–1384.

Williams, Yvonne. (1999, July/August). Amy and Mr. Matthews. Colorado Springs, Colorado. *Bereavement Magazine,* pp. 22–23.

Wolfelt, A.D. (1990a, February). Adolescent mourning, a naturally complicated experience, Part I. *Bereavement Magazine,* pp. 34–35.

Wolfelt, A.D. (1990b, March/April). Adolescent mourning, a naturally complicated experience, Part II. *Bereavement Magazine,* pp. 34–35.

Books for Adults and Older Teens

Bernstein, Joanne. (1977). *Loss and how to cope with it.* New York: Seabury Press.

Bode, Janet. (1994). *Death is hard to live with.* New York: Delacorte.

Cole, Diane. (1992). *After great pain, a new life emerges.* New York: Summit Books.

Donnelly, Katherine Fair. (1988). *Recovering from the loss of a sibling.* New York: Dodd, Mead.

Donnelly, Katherine Fair. (1993). *Recovering from the loss of a parent.* New York: Berkley.

Frankl, Viktor E. (1984). *Man's search for meaning: An introduction to logotherapy* (3rd ed.). New York: Simon & Schuster.

Kübler-Ross, Elisabeth. (1969). *On death and dying.* New York: Macmillan.

Kübler-Ross, Elisabeth. (1982). *Working it through.* New York: Macmillan.

Lord, Janice Harris. (1987). *No time for good-byes: Coping with sorrow, anger and injustice after a tragic death.* Ventura, CA: Pathfinder.

Lord, Janice Harris. (1992). *Beyond sympathy: What to say and do for someone suffering an injury, illness or loss.* Ventura, CA: Pathfinder.

Martin, Terry L., & Doka, Kenneth J. (2000) *Men don't cry . . . women do: Transcending gender stereotypes of grief.* Philadelphia, PA: Taylor & Francis.

Prend, Ashley. (1997). *Transcending loss.* New York: Berkley Books.

Stearns, Ann Kaiser. (1984). *Living through personal crisis.* New York: Ballantine Books.

Stearns, Ann Kaiser. (1988). *Coming back: Rebuilding lives after crisis and loss.* New York: Random House.

Tatelbaum, Judy. (1980). *The courage to grieve.* New York: Harper & Row.

Viorst, Judith. (1986). *Necessary losses.* New York: Simon & Schuster.

Books Specifically Related to Trauma

Alexander, Debera Whiting. (1999). *Children changed by trauma: A healing guide.* Oakland, CA: New Harbinger.

Doka, Kenneth J. (1996). *Living with grief after sudden loss.* Philadelphia, PA: Taylor & Francis.

Figley, Charles R. (Ed.). (1999). *Traumatology of grieving: Conceptual, theoretical, and treatment foundations.* Philadelphia, PA: Taylor & Francis.

Gordon, Norma S., Farberow, Norman L., & Maida, Carl A. (1999). *Children and disasters*. Philadelphia, PA: Taylor & Francis.

Herman, Judith. (1997). *Trauma and recovery: The aftermath of violence—From domestic abuse to political terror*. New York: Basic Books.

Johnson, Kendall. (1998). *Trauma in the lives of children: Crisis and stress management techniques for counselors, teachers, and other professionals* (2nd ed.). Alameda, CA: Hunter House.

Johnson, Kendall. (1993). *School crisis management: A hands-on guide to training crisis response teams*. Alameda, CA: Hunter House.

Kauffman, Jeffrey (Ed.). (2002). *Loss of the assumptive world: A theory of traumatic loss*. New York: Brunner-Routledge.

Lattanzi-Licht, Marcia, & Doka, Kenneth J. (Eds.). (2003). *Coping with public tragedy*. New York: Brunner-Routledge.

Materials That Include Spiritual Aspects

Campbell, Peter, & McMahon, Edwin. (1997). *Bio-spirituality: Focusing as a way to grow*. Chicago: Loyola Press.

Coles, Robert. (1990). *The spiritual life of children*. Boston: A Peter Davison Book.

Doka, Kenneth. (2002). How could God? Loss and the spiritual assumptive world. In Jeffrey Kauffman (Ed.), *Loss of the assumptive world: A theory of traumatic loss* (pp. 49–54). New York: Brunner-Routedge.

Hewett, John H. (1980). *After suicide*. Philadelphia: Westminster Press.

Kennedy, Alexandra. (1997). *Your loved one lives within you*. New York: Berkley Books.

Krauss, Pesach, & Goldfischer, Morrie. (1988). *Why me?: Coping with grief, loss, and change*. New York: Bantam Books.

Kuenning, Delores. (1987). *Helping people through grief*. Minneapolis: Bethany House.

Kushner, Harold S. (1981). *When bad things happen to good people*. New York: Avon Books.

Manning, Doug. 1984. *Don't take my grief away: What to do when you lose a loved one*. New York: Harper & Row.

Nouwen, Henri J. M. (1982). *A letter of consolation*. New York: HarperCollins.

Prend, Ashley Davis. (1997). *Transcending loss: Understanding the lifelong impact of grief and how to make it meaningful*. New York: Berkley Books.

Rupp, Joyce. (1988). *Praying our goodbyes*. New York: Ivy Books.

Wolff, Pierre. (1979). *May I hate God?* New York: Paulist Press.

VIDEOS

Braza, Kathleen. (1995). *To touch a grieving heart: Healing ways to help ourselves and others walk the journey of grief.* Salt Lake City: Panacom Incorporated. Grief counselor and certified thanatologist Kathleen Braza talks about the complex array of emotions that are often confusing and painful to the bereaved person, and what to say and not say when offering support.

Children and trauma: The school's response. (1990). Directed by Eric Thiermann and Mark Schwartz. Order through Impact Productions, 1725B Seabright Ave, Santa Cruz, CA 95062.

Pikes Peak Hospice. (1993). *Saying goodbye: Teens sharing stories of grief and loss* (teen edition). Medfield, MA: Aquarius Health Care Videos (34 minutes). Bereaved teens share their pain and growth after the loss of a loved one.

Pikes Peak Hospice. (1993). *Saying goodbye: Teens sharing stories of grief and loss* (teacher edition). Medfield, MA: Aquarius Health Care Videos (34 minutes). Bereaved teens share their pain and growth after the loss of a loved one; explanations directed at adults are included.

Schwiebert, Pat, & DeKlyen, Chuck. (2003). *Tear soup: A recipe for healing after loss.* This video can be purchased at www.griefwatch.com.

Tatelbaum, Judith. (1994). *The courage to grieve, the courage to grow.* Medfield, MA: Aquarius Health Care Videos (45 minutes). Renowned grief specialist describes the stages of grief and tools for healing.

White, Cynthia, & Spencer, Don. (1994). *Facilitating teens in grief.* Portland, Oregon: Dougy Center. A teen grief group is followed effectively from beginning to end, providing an effective tool for facilitators of teen groups.

Wolfelt, Alan. (1997). *A teen's view of grief: An educational videotape for bereavement caregivers.* Fort Collins, CO: Companion Press (40 minutes). This tape provides practical guidelines for accompanying teens on their journey of grief.

POSTER

Grief art project. (1992). For information write: Carol Lobell, 10523 Tolling Clock Way, Columbia, MD 21044. This project shows stages of grief in a graphic form, and is available in various sizes.

MEDIA SERVICES AND CLEARINGHOUSES

Centering Corporation. Omaha, NE. 402-553-1200 www.centering.org

Compassion Book Service. Burnesville, NC. 828-675-5909 www.compassionbooks.com

Companion Press. Fort Collins, CO. 970-226-0605 www.centerforloss.com

Aquarius Health Care Videos. Medfield, MA 888-440-2963 www.aquariusproductions.com

ORGANIZATIONS

American Association of Suicidology (AAS)
4201 Connecticut Ave. NW
Suite 408
Washington, DC 20008
202-237-2280
www.suicidology.org

American Trauma Society
8903 Presidential Parkway
Suite 512
Upper Marlboro, MD 20772
1-800-556-7890 or 301-420-4189
www.amtrauma.org
E-mail: info@amtrauma.org

Association for Death Education and Counseling (ADEC)
432 North Main St.
West Hartford, CT 06117-2507
860-586-7503
www.adec.org
E-mail: info@adec.org
The Association for Death Education and Counseling provides information on both theory and research, support, and resources to professionals.

Association of Traumatic Stress Specialists (ATSS)
7338 Broad River Rd.
Irmo, SC 29063
803-781-0017
www.atts-hq.com
The Association of Traumatic Stress Specialists is an international nonprofit organization dedicated to providing certification and professional education to professionals involved in trauma response, treatment, management, and crisis organization. ATSS maintains an international list of skilled professionals in the areas of crisis response, training, and therapy.

Bereavement Services (formerly Resolve Through Sharing)
Gunderson Lutheran Medical Foundation
1910 South Ave.
LaCrosse, WI 54601
608-775-4747
1-800-362-9567, ext. 54747
www.bereavementprograms.com

Center for Loss and Grief Therapy
10400 Connecticut Ave.
Suite 514
Kensington, MD 20985
301-942-6440
www.erols.com/lgold

Center for Loss and Life Transitions
3735 Broken Bow Rd.
Fort Collins, CO 80526
970-226-6050
www.centerforloss.com

Children's Hospice International
901 North Pitt St.
Suite 230
Alexandria, VA 22314
703-684-0330 or 1-800-2-4-CHILD

Compassionate Friends, Inc.
National Headquarters
PO Box 3696
Chicago, IL 60522-3696
630-990-0010
877-969-0010 (Toll-free)
www.compassionatefriends.org
Compassionate Friends is a self-help organization that offers friendship and understanding to parents and families following the death of a child. They provide booklets and pamphlets as well as information on local chapters.

Dougy Center
PO Box 86852
Portland, OR 97286
503-775-5683
www.grievingchild.org
E-mail: help@dougy.org
The Dougy Center provides national training and consultations to schools and organizations, as well as support groups for grieving children and teens.

Fernside, A Center for Grieving Children
2303 Indian Mound Ave.
Cincinnati, OH 45212
513-841-1012
www.fernside.org

Hospice Foundation of America
2001 S Street, NW
Suite 300
Washington, DC 20009
800-854-3402
www.hospicefoundation.org
E-mail: hfa@hospicefoundation.org
Hospice Foundation of America is a not-for-profit organization that provides leadership in the development and application of hospice and its philosophy of care. The foundation produces an annual award-winning National Bereavement Teleconference and publishes the Living With Grief book series in conjunction with the teleconference.

Hospice Information Service
51–59 Lawrie Park Road
Sydenham
London SE26 6DZ; United Kingdom
Tel: 0870 903 3 903
www.hospiceinformation.info/
Directory of Hospice Services with details of hospices in many areas is available. Most hospices have bereavement groups; some have groups for teens.

Institute for BioSpiritual Research
(as developed by Edwin M. McMahon, PhD, & Peter A. Campbell, PhD)
Attn: Loretta Flom
PO Box 741137
Arvada, CO 80006-1137
Telephone/fax: 303-427-5311
www.biospiritual.org

International Critical Incident Stress Foundation
3290 Pine Orchard Lane, Suite 106
Ellicott City, MD 21042
410-750-9600
24-hour hotline 410-313-2473
www.icisf.org

Kids in Crisis
1 Salem Street
Cos Cob, CT 06807
203-622-6556
www.kidsincrisis.org

Kidspeace National Center for Kids in Crisis
5300 KidsPeace Dr.
Orefield, PA 18069
1-800-8KID-123 or 1-800-344-4KID
www.kidspeace.org

Motherless Daughters, Inc.
PO Box 663
Prince Street Station
New York, NY 10012
212-614-8041

NAMES Project
310 Townsend St., Suite 310
San Francisco, CA 94107
415-882-5500
www.AIDSQuilt.org
E-mail: Info@AIDSQuilt.com

National AIDS Information Clearinghouse (AIDSinfo)
PO Box 6303
Rockville, MD 20850
1-800-HIV-0440
www.aidsinfo.nih.gov

National Association for Victim Assistance (NOVA)
1730 Park Rd., NW
Washington, DC 20010
202-232-6682
(Information/Referral Line) 800-TRY-NOVA
NOVA is an organization that provides advocacy and assistance to people who have lost friends and family through murder. It also provides information on local chapters.

National Hospice Organization
1700 Diagonal Road, Suite 625
Alexandria, VA 22314
703-837-1500 or 1-800-646-6460
www.nhpco.org
E-mail: nhpco_info@nhcpo.org
The National Hospice Organization provides the general public and healthcare professionals with information about hospice and palliative care, reimbursement sources, and referrals to local hospice programs throughout the United States.

National Victim Center
2111 Wilson Blvd.
Suite 300
Arlington, VA 22201
703-276-2880

National Center for Victims of Crime
2000 M Street NW Suite 480
Washington, DC 20036
202-467-8700
E-mail: webmaster@ncvc.org
The National Center for Victims of Crime is a nonprofit organization providing resource and advocacy for victims of crime in the U.S.

New England Center for Loss and Transition (NECLT)
PO Box 292
Guilford, CT 06437-0292
1-800-887-5677
www.neclt.org
E-mail: staff@neclt.org
NECLT is a nonprofit organization dedicated to training professionals in the field of bereavement, grief, and loss.

Rainbows
2100 Golf Road #307
Rolling Meadows, IL 60008-4231
1-800-266-3206
www.rainbows.org
Rainbows provides resources designed to foster emotional healing among children grieving a loss from a life-altering crisis.

SIDS Alliance (formerly National Sudden Infant Death Syndrome Foundation)
1314 Bedford Ave.
Suite 210
Baltimore, MD 21208
1-800-221-SIDS or 410-653-8226
www.sidsalliance.org

Survivors of Suicide
Suicide Prevention Center
184 Salem Ave.
Dayton, OH 45406
513-223-9096

Teen Age Grief, Inc. (TAG)
PO Box 220034
Newhall, CA 91322-0034
661-253-1932
www.smartlink.net/~tag/
Teen Age Grief (TAG) is a nonprofit organization that provides education and practical ideas to individuals working with teens individually or in a support-group setting. Training manuals, activity books, audiocassettes, and videos are some of the material available for purchase.

Youth Suicide National Center
1825 Eye Street, NW
Suite 400
Washington, DC 20006
202-429-2016

HOTLINES

Boys Town National Crisis Hotline	800-448-3000
	800-448-1833 (hearing impaired)
Covenant House Nineline	800-999-9999
Grief Recovery Helpline	800-445-4808
Hospice Helpline	800-658-8898
Kid Save	800-543-7283
National Runaway Switchboard	800-621-4000 or 800-231-6946
Primary Health Management Systems	800-444-9999
Youth Crisis Hot Line	800-HIT-HOME

ADDITIONAL WEBSITES

www.bereavementmag.com: Through this website of *Bereavement Magazine,* anyone can create a free e-memorial, or send an e-sympathy message, browse magazine articles, subjects, books, cards, gifts, and videos. Grants permission to reprint all articles, provided the magazine is credited.

www.compassionatefriends.org: This website is designed to help families (parents, siblings, relatives) after the death of a child. Compassionate Friends is a not-for-profit support organization with no religious affiliations.

www.erols.com/lgold: Linda Goldman's website, Helping Children Dealing with Grief, highlights helpful books, articles, and information about children and grief. The site includes a special section on terrorism and trauma for parents and children.

www.fernside.org/: Fernside is a nondenominational organization specifically geared toward grieving children and their families. It has two main sections, one specifically for children and the other specifically for their families. It contains lists of grief centers around the country as well as printed and online resources.

www.griefnet.org: Griefnet provides information and resources about support groups and professionals offering services and products. Formerly www.rivendell.org

www.griefrecovery.com: Grief Share describes how to develop an outreach program. This is a site where you can search for local grief groups. This is a nondenominational Christian organization that incorporates biblical teaching on grief topics.

www.griefsheart.com: This opportunity to share stories from the Heart of Grief and Stories of Grief after September 11 is managed by Tom Attig.

www.griefwatch.com: Grief Watch provides bereavement resources, memorial products, and links to other resources for the bereaved and caregivers. The popular book and video, both entitled *Tear Soup: A Recipe for Healing After Loss*, along with other grief-related materials, are available for purchase.

www.kidsaid.com: KidSaid is an interactive website for children and adults. The site includes questions and answers for children and adults, poetry, games, stories, and lists of support groups. It is a place designed for children to help each other with their grief.

www.madd.org: This website, run by Mothers Against Drunk Driving (MADD), provides resources and information for injured victims and bereaved persons due to a drunk driving crash. You can view tributes, submit a tribute of your own, and read other people's stories.

www.motivateus.com: Motivating Moments is an on-line collection of inspirational quotes, including a section "By teens and for teens" and a section "Helping through the grief."

www.npr.org/programs/death/resources.html: This website, entitled "The End of Life: Exploring Death in America," offers lists of websites and organizations compiled by the staff of National Public Radio's *All Things Considered.*

www.thesanctuaryforgrief.org: Services provided by The Sanctuary include crisis response and debriefing, school personnel training, corporate personnel training, bereavement education seminars, bereavement support groups, and individual grief counseling for adults and children.

References

Alexander, Debra. (1999). *Children changed by trauma: A healing guide.* Oakland, CA: New Harbinger Publications.

Allen, Kathy, Perschy, Mary, & Richardson, Mary. (2002, October–December). Gathering grieving families: Three activities. *The Forum,* pp. 6–7.

Attig, Tom. (2000). *The heart of grief.* New York: Oxford University Press.

Balk, D. E. (1991). Sibling death, adolescence: Self-concept & bereavement reactions. *Death Studies, 15,* 1–20, 1991.

Balk, D. E. (1999). Bereavement and spiritual change. *Death Studies, 23*(6), 485–493.

Be aware of the warning signs. (2002, March). *Some facts about suicide and depression.* Washington, DC: American Association of Suicidology.

Bowlby, John. (1978). Attachment theory and its therapeutic implications. *Adolescent Psychiatry, 6,* 5–33.

Campbell, Peter, & McMahon, Edwin. (1991). *The focusing steps.* New York: Sheed and Ward.

Cobb, S. (1976). Social support as a moderator of life stress. *Psychosomatic Medicine, 38*(5), 300–314.

Coles, Robert. (1990). *The spiritual life of children.* Boston: Houghton Mifflin.

Corr, Charles A., & McNeil, J. N. (1986). *Adolescence and death.* New York: Springer.

Corr, Charles A., Nabe, Clyde M., & Corr, Donna M. (2000). *Death and dying, life and living* (3rd ed.). Belmont, CA: Wadsworth/Thomson Learning.

Doka, Kenneth. (2002). How could God? Loss and the spiritual assumptive world. In Jeffrey Kauffman (Ed.), *Loss of the assumptive world: A theory of traumatic loss* (pp. 49–54). New York: Brunner-Routedge.

Dower, Laura. (2001). *I will remember you: What to do when someone you love dies: A guidebook through grief for teens.* New York: Scholastic, Inc.

Fleming, S. J., & Adolph, R. (1986). Helping bereaved adolescents. In C. Corr & J. McNeil (Eds.), *Adolescence and death* (pp. 97–118). New York: Springer.

Frank, Stephanie. (2000, September 26). My mind, emotions and soul matured . . . too fast for my years. *The Washington Post,* p. C1.

Frankl, Viktor E. (1984). *Man's search for meaning: An introduction to logotherapy* (3rd ed.). New York: Simon & Schuster.

Gamino, Louis A. (2003). Critical incident stress management and other crisis counseling approaches. In Marcia Lattanzi-Licht & Kenneth J. Doka (Eds.), *Coping with public tragedy* (pp. 123–138). New York: Hospice Foundation and Brunner-Routledge.

Goldman, Linda. (1996). *Breaking the silence: A guide to help children with complicated grief—Suicide, homicide, AIDS, violence, and abuse*. Washington, DC: Taylor & Francis.

Goldman, Linda. (2002). The assumptive world of children. In Jeffrey Kauffman (Ed.). *Loss of the assumptive world: A theory of traumatic loss*. (pp. 193–202). New York: Brunner-Routledge.

Gray, Ross E. (1988, January). The role of school counselors with bereaved teenagers: With and without peer support groups. *The School Counselor*. pp. 185–193.

Hipp, Earl. (1995). *Help for the hard times: Getting through loss*. Center City, MN: Hazelden.

Hogan, Nancy S., & DeSantis, Lydia (1994). Things that help and hinder adolescent sibling bereavement. *Western Journal of Nursing Research, 16*(2), 132–153.

Hogan, Nancy S., & Greenfield, Daryl B. (1991, January). Adolescent sibling bereavement symptomatology in a large community sample. *Journal of Adolescent Research, 6*(1), 97–112.

Jacobsen, Gail B. (1990). *Write grief: How to transform loss through writing*. Menomonee Falls, WI: McCormick and Schilling.

Johnson, Spencer. (1984). *The precious present.* New York: Doubleday.

Klass, D., Silverman, P., & Nickman, S. (1996). *Continuing bonds*. Philadelphia: Taylor & Francis

Merritt, Stephanie. (1996). *Mind, music and imagery.* Santa Rosa, CA: Aslan Publishing.

Morse, Jodie. (2002). The 9/11 kid. *Time South Pacific, 35*, 40–49.

Moss, M. S., & Moss, S.Z. (1989). *The death of a parent.* In R. A. Kalish (Ed.) *Midlife loss: Coping strategies* (pp. 89–114). Newbury Park, CA: Sage.

Normand, Claude L., Silverman, P. R., & Nickman, Steven. (1996). Bereaved children's changing relationships with the deceased. In D. Klass, P. R. Silverman, & S. L. Nickman (Eds.), *Continuing bonds* (pp. 87–112). Philadelphia: Taylor & Francis.

Oltjenbruns, Kevin Ann. (1991). Positive outcomes of adolescents' experience with grief. *Journal of Adolescent Research, 6*(1), 43–53.

Perschy, Mary K. (1989, Winter). Crazy grief. *To Make the Road Less Lonely,* pp. 1, 3. Columbia, MD: Hospice Services of Howard County.

Perschy, Mary, & Barker, Anne. (1990, June). Teen grief group: Respite from isolation. *Bereavement Magazine*, pp. 42–43.

Prend, Ashley. (1997). *Transcending loss.* New York: Berkley Books.

Rando, Therese A. (1996). Complications in mourning traumatic death. In Ken Doka (Ed.), *Living with grief after sudden loss: Suicide, homicide, accident, heart attack, stroke* (pp. 139–160). Bristol, PA: Taylor & Francis.

Rando, Therese A. (2003). Public tragedy and complicated mourning. In Marcia Lattanzi-Licht & Ken Doka (Eds.), *Living with grief: Coping with public tragedy* (pp. 263–274). New York: Brunner-Routledge.

Rizzuto, A. M. (1979). *The birth of the living God: A psychoanalytic study.* Chicago: University of Chicago Press.

Silverman, Phyllis R., & Nickman, Steven. (1996). Children's construction of their dead parents. In D. Klass, P. R. Silverman, & S. L. Nickman (Eds). *Continuing bonds* (pp. 73–86). Philadelphia: Taylor & Francis.

Silverman, Phyllis, R., & Worden, J. William. (1992). Children's reactions in the early months after the death of a parent. *American Journal of Orthopsychiatry, 62*(1), 93–104.

Simons, R. C. (1985). *Understanding human behavior in health and illness* (3rd ed.) Baltimore, MD: Lippincott Williams & Wilkins.

Steele, James M. (2002). *Sadie listens.* Glenwood Springs, CO: Steele Studios Publishing Division.

Tatelbaum, J. (1980). *The courage to grieve.* New York: HarperCollins.

Tubesing, Nancy, & Tubesing, Donald. (1983). Goodbye means ouch! In *The stress examiner.* Duluth, MN: Whole Press Associates, in cooperation with Aid Association for Lutherans.

Vachon, M., & Stylianos, K. (1988). The role of social support in bereavement. *Journal of Social Issues, 44,* 175–190.

Vachon, M. L. S., Lyall, W. A. L., Rogers, J., Freedman-Leftofsky, K., & Freedman, S. J. J. (1980). A controlled study of self-help intervention for widows. *American Journal of Psychiatry, 137,* 1380–1384.

Wolf, Anthony E. (1991). *Get out of my life, but first could you drive me and Cheryl to the mall: A parent's guide to the new teenager.* New York: Noonday Press.

Wolfelt, A. D. (1990a, February). Adolescent mourning, a naturally complicated experience, Part I. *Bereavement Magazine,* pp. 34–35.

Wolfelt, A.D. (1990b, March/April). Adolescent mourning, a naturally complicated experience, Part II. *Bereavement Magazine,* pp. 34–35.

Wolfelt, Alan. (2001a). *Healing your grieving heart for teens.* Fort Collins, CO: Companion Press.

Wolfelt, Alan D. (2001b). *Healing a teen's grieving heart: 100 Practical ideas for families, friends and caregivers.* Fort Collins, CO: Companion Press.

Worden, J. William. (1996). *Children and grief.* New York: Guilford Press.

Worden, J. William. (2002). *Grief counseling and grief therapy: A handbook for the mental health practitioner* (3rd ed.). New York: Springer.

About the Author

Mary Perschy believes that grief can be a transforming process for those who are willing to enter into the mystery of the experience. In her seventeen years as a facilitator of grief groups, especially groups for teens, she is convinced of the value of accompanying teens in a group setting.

She now recognizes that her enthusiasm for encouraging such support springs from her personal story of wrestling with the feelings of grief as a teen herself when her mother died from cancer. Years later, when she completed her counseling degree from Johns Hopkins University, she was drawn into hospice work, where she began working with bereaved teens.

Perschy has more recently been trained in spiritual direction through the Shalem Institute in Bethesda, Maryland. She continues to explore the spiritual dimension in every aspect of living. This exploration has naturally been a part of her work with those who grieve.

She lives with her husband, Jim, in Maryland.

Index